C000178334

William Morris
on History

William MORRIS

on History

edited by Nicholas Salmon

Sheffield
Academic Press

Copyright © 1996 Sheffield Academic Press

Published by Sheffield Academic Press Ltd
Mansion House
19 Kingfield Road
Sheffield S11 9AS
England

Printed on acid-free paper in Great Britain
by The Cromwell Press
Melksham, Wiltshire

British Library Cataloguing in Publication Data

A catalogue record for this book is available
from the British Library

ISBN 1-85075-606-6

CONTENTS

CONTENTS

INTRODUCTION

Williiam Morris was one of the most prolific writers of the Victorian Age. During the last twenty years of his life he composed and delivered over one hundred lectures, contributed nearly five hundred articles to socialist journals such as *Justice* and *Commonweal*, and wrote numerous manifestos and pamphlets for organizations that ranged from the Society for the Protection of Ancient Buildings to his own Socialist League. This was in addition to a body of creative writing that included poetry, translations, dialogues, drama and prose romances. The quality and perception of these works have quite rightly established him as one of the foremost nineteenth-century commentators on art, design and socialism.

What is less well known is that Morris was also a historian of considerable ability. A central element in all his creative work was an extensive knowledge of the past. This can be detected in all his writing from the poetry of *The Earthly Paradise* (1868-70) to the prose romances he wrote in the last years of his life. It also informed his critique of capitalism and served as the basis for many of the lectures he delivered following his conversion to socialism in 1883. The aim of this volume is to gather together for the first time the most important of Morris's writings on history in order to facilitate a reassessment of this sadly neglected aspect of his work.

There are two reasons why Morris's historical writings have been overlooked. The first is that the manuscripts of many of his lectures on historical subjects have been lost. According to

Eugene LeMire these include 'Iceland: Its Ancient Literature and Mythology' (1884), 'Slaves and Slave Holders' (1885), 'The Guilds of the Middle Ages' (1885), 'The Birth of Feudalism in Scandinavia' (1886) and 'From Chattel to Wage Slavery' (1888).[1] Perhaps the greatest loss is the text of a lecture Morris gave before the Hammersmith Branch of the Socialist League in 1888 entitled '"A Chapter in the History of Rome": A Lecture on Theodore Mommsen'. Morris had first read Mommsen's *History of Rome* in 1875 and he re-read the book in preparation for his lecture in August 1888. The loss of his detailed observations on the organization of society during the classical age is much to be regretted.

The other problem has been that the historical writings that have survived have not been easily accessible to the general reader. Of the five lectures included in the present volume only three—'The Hopes of Civilization' (1885), 'Feudal England' (1887) and 'Art and Industry in the 14th Century' (1887)—were included in *The Collected Works of William Morris*. 'Early England' (1886), the first lecture in a trilogy Morris gave on the subject 'England, As It Was, As It Is, and As It May Be', remained in manuscript form until 1969 when Eugene LeMire included it in his *The Unpublished Lectures of William Morris*. 'The Development of Modern Society' (1890) has not been published in its entirety since it was serialized in Morris's socialist newspaper *Commonweal*.[2] The historical chapters of *Socialism from the Root Up* were also omitted from *The Collected Works*, as were most of the articles Morris contributed to nineteenth-century socialist journals.

Three important influences can be traced on the historical writings that have survived. The first of these was Morris's life-long interest in the Middle Ages. This began as a child when he rode around the grounds of his parents' house in Essex dressed in a miniature suit of armour. By the time he went to Oxford University in 1853 it had developed into something of an obsession and he read every book he could find on the subject.

Amongst the works he read in this context were those of the early chroniclers such as Froissart and Holinshed. However, his interest in medieval history was most profoundly affected by the new tradition in social criticism, characterized by books like Carlyle's *Past and Present* (1843) and Ruskin's *The Stones of Venice* (1851-53), which used the achievements of the Middle Ages as the basis for an attack on contemporary society. E.P. Thompson has claimed that the most important result of this new scholarship for Morris was its 'reconstruction of a picture of the Middle Ages, neither as a grotesque nor as a faery world, but as a real *community* of human beings—an organic pre-capitalist community with values and an art of its own, sharply contrasted with those of Victorian England'.[3] Thompson went on to add that in 'this reconstructed world, Morris found a place, not to which he could retreat, but in which he could stand and look upon his own age with the eyes of a stranger or visitor, judging his own time by standards other than his own'.[4] It was this technique of juxtaposing an idealized vision of the Middle Ages with the misery and corruption of capitalist society that characterized most of Morris's early lectures on art and labour.

Following his conversion to socialism, two further influences helped shape Morris's mature view of the evolution of human civilization. As part of the background research for his historical lectures he became interested in the lives of the early Teutonic peoples and the influence of their tribal practices on the development of modern British institutions. May Morris recorded that in the mid-1880s this period of history came to have 'a great fascination for ... [her father], who read with critical enjoyment the more important studies of it as they came out'.[5] Amanda Hodgson has claimed that Morris was familiar with a tradition in English historical scholarship which began in 1768 with Gilbert Stuart's *An Historical Dissertation Concerning the Antiquity of the English Constitution*, and then continued through Sharon Turner's *History of the Anglo-Saxons* (1799-1805), Kemble's *The Saxons in*

England (1849), William Stubb's *The Constitutional History of England in its Origin and Development* (1874-78), John Richard Green's *A Short History of the English People* (1874: but reprinted in a revised form in 1888) and the radical historian Edward A. Freeman's *The History of the Norman Conquest of England* (1867-79).[6] Elsewhere, John Goode has suggested that Morris had also read the American historian Lewis H. Morgan's *Ancient Society, or Researches in the Lines of Human Progress from Savagery through Barbarism to Civilisation* which was published in England in 1877.[7]

Morris had certainly read the work of Freeman and Green as he mentioned both men as examples of 'the new school of historians' in 'The Revival of Architecture', an article published in the *Fortnightly Review* in 1888.[8] There are also isolated references to other works. The most important of these occurs in 'Early England' where Morris relied heavily on Charles Elton's *The Origins of English History* (1882). In the same lecture he also mentioned Benjamin Thorpe's edition of *The Anglo-Saxon Chronicles* which was published in 1861. Elsewhere, in 'The Early Literature of the North—Iceland' (1887), Morris referred to G.W. Dasent's article 'The Norsemen in Iceland' which had appeared in *Oxford Essays* published in London in 1858. This suggests that he was also familiar with Dasent's history of Iceland. Dasent's work would have supplemented Morris's already extensive knowledge of the Icelandic Sagas.

However, the crucial influence on Morris's historical writings of the 1880s was his reading of the works of the new school of scientific socialists. He was particularly impressed by Volume I of Marx's *Das Kapital* which he read in French in 1883. Marx's analysis of the origins of capitalism introduced Morris to the concept of class consciousness and provided him with a dialectical framework within which to explore his own ideas about the past history of human civilization. It also provided him with a message of hope for the future. As he wrote in 'The Hopes of Civilization', the greatest achievement of Karl Marx and the scientific socialists was that by 'starting with an historical view of what had been, and seeing that a law of evolution swayed all events in it, [they were] ... able to point out to us that the evolution was still going on, and that, whether socialism be desirable or not, it is at least inevitable' (p. 44). In *Socialism from the Root Up* Morris cited amongst the other important works of scientific socialism Marx and Engels' *The Holy Family* (1844), their *Manifesto of the Communist Party* (1847-48) and Marx's *The Eighteenth Brumaire of Louis Bonaparte* (1852). It is also possible that he was familiar with Engels's *The Origin of the Family, Private Property and the State* (1884).

Morris's own ideas about the development of early human society—what he considered to be the first great epoch in history—are to be found in his lectures 'Early England' and 'The Development of Modern Society', and in Chapter I of *Socialism from the Root Up* entitled 'Ancient Society'. In the latter collaboration with E. Belfort Bax, Morris identified three stages in the early evolution of humanity: savagery, barbarism and ancient civilization. Of these three he paid the least attention to the period of savagery, merely introducing it as a condition of anarchy in which all human actions were determined by the need to satisfy basic animal desires. As a result there was no co-operation between individuals and no formal social organization of any kind.

Morris argued that this state of savagery only gradually gave way to barbarism. This process began when people developed basic agricultural skills which enabled them to produce more food and goods than were needed for their immediate survival. In pursuing these new skills people were drawn together into small groups where individual self-gratification was replaced by a form of primitive communism in which all people were equal. This was possible—in the early days at least—because all property belonged to the community and the concept of private ownership did not exist. According to Morris, barbarism itself evolved through three stages: the Gens, the Tribe and the People. Although these stages were by no means mutually exclusive, Morris believed an understanding of the process by which the Gens was transformed into the People was crucial in explaining the nature of the second great epoch in history—that of feudalism.

The Gens, or clan, was the basic unit of social organization during the earliest period of barbarism. Each Gens consisted of 'a group of blood relations at peace amongst themselves' but hostile to all outside groups. (p. 145) Within the Gens all bond-pairing was exogamous. Inter-marriage between members was forbidden and wives had to be found outside the Gens. In 'The Development of Modern Society', Morris went on to argue—as Engels and Morgan had done—that at first the Gens were matriarchal in organization, with descent being traced through the mother. Within the Gens wealth was held in common, but outside all wealth was regarded as a prize of war. This condition of perpetual war developed leadership qualities amongst men with the result that as time went on 'successful warriors gained prominence over the other members of the *Gens*' (p. 145). As the wealth of the Gens increased above that needed for mere survival these warriors began to gain an increasingly large share of the collective wealth. This in turn marked the point where 'the primitive communism of wealth began to be transformed into individual ownership' (p. 145). Eventually, due to the rule banning marriage within a single blood-related Gens, groups of Gens began to amalgamate together in order to facilitate procreation. By this means the individual Gens were gradually superseded by the wider concept of the Tribe.

Morris claimed that the Tribe was a larger and more artificial association in which blood relations were only conventionally assumed. Nevertheless, as a result of this bonding—in which all members were deemed to have 'a common ancestor' who was worshipped as a god—there was no war between the clans or

Gens who composed the Tribe. Similarly, although elements of the individual ownership developed in the Gens remained, there was a communal responsibility within the Tribe for disposing of and cultivating the land. The most significant development was that it was during the middle stage of barbarism that the practice of slavery first began. This in turn marked the first discernible movement towards class society.

In the final stage of barbarism the Tribe eventually melted into a larger and still more artificial grouping: the People. The People, Morris wrote in *Socialism from the Root Up*, was a grouping of many tribes 'the ancient Gothic-Teutonic name for which—theoth—is still preserved in such names as *Theo*bald' (p. 146). These tribes were still bound by the idea that they were derived from common ancestors and therefore shared collective kinship through their worship of the same gods. Despite the more loose-knit nature of this arrangement there was little change in the condition of wealth to that pertaining within the Tribe. Nevertheless, Morris considered this to be the final stage in the development of barbarism before it melted into feudalism. In its later stages it therefore contained what Morris termed 'something more than the mere *germs* of feudalism' (p. 146).

These '*germs*' of feudalism' originated in the form of slavery that emerged during the later stages of barbarism. As tribal life was characterized by a state of perpetual war it was inevitable that sooner or later the question of what to do with prisoners taken in battle had to be addressed. Under classical civilization the problem was solved by the development of chattel slavery. However, in the case of the Germanic tribes the process proved to be more complex due to their relatively primitive ideas concerning individual ownership of property. Indeed, in the early stages of barbarism the defeated tribesmen were actually adopted into the kindred. As time went on, however, the defeated tribes became so large that it was no longer possible to assimilate the numbers involved. Defeated tribes were therefore obliged to farm their lands for the benefit of their conquerors in exchange for military protection. According to Morris it was from this practice, along with the growth of individual wealth amongst the chieftains, that the whole complex feudal hierarchy of the Middle Ages was to evolve.

While barbarism was undergoing these developments it existed alongside a new and parallel form of social organization, that of ancient civilization. Classical society, Morris claimed in 'The Development of Modern Society', was 'founded on the corruption of the society of the tribes by the institution of private property' (p. 114). While in the earliest period—in both Greece and Rome—the tribal ideal of the merging of the individual into the community was still strong, it was soon to give way to the rise in individualism which accompanied the creation of private property. Before long the idea of the community became merely an abstraction and no longer served as 'the real visible body of persons ... [to which] individual interests were to be sacrificed' (p. 111). This abstraction was most apparent amongst the Romans in their worship of the city. Nevertheless, Morris argued that at first this was not an entirely negative feature as it encouraged the idea of a 'public spirit' which manifested itself in the construction of noble buildings. It was only over time that the old communal ideals became corrupted into 'an inflexible central authority idealized into a religion and symbolized in the person of the emperor, the master of the world enthroned in an Italian city'.[9]

This deterioration in communal values was accompanied by the gradual development of slavery. Under barbarism the slaves at first formed only a small part of the work force and most productive labour was undertaken by the tribespeople themselves. This continued in a relatively similar fashion during the early period of ancient civilization—both in Greece and Rome— where, as he put it in 'The Development of Modern Society', 'a great deal of the field-work was done by the freemen; the

family [only being] ... helped in it by the slaves' (p. 112).
However, Morris claimed that as society grew richer the occupations fell more and more under the division of labour system.
This meant that 'slave labour increased very much, till in the last days of the Roman republic the proportions of slaves to free labour relative to the handicrafts and agriculture had quite changed' (p. 113). In effect the slaves, like the proletariat under capitalism, had become the only producers of wealth.

Accompanying this redistribution of work was a corresponding, but gradual, redistribution of ownership in the means of production. In the early days of ancient civilization the ownership of the land 'had been common ... and the *use* divided amongst the citizens' (p. 113). However, as the practice of slavery developed, the land increasingly came into the hands of larger and larger landlords with the result that all productive labour came to be done by slaves. This polarization—which Morris once again compared to that between the proletariat and bourgeoisie under capitalism—had two important consequences. On the one hand the despair and hopelessness of the slaves began to manifest itself in open rebellion. Morris cited in particular the great slave mutiny led by Spartacus, but also mentioned the 'countless minor mutinies by sea and land' that tormented the Empire during its final years. On the other hand the rich became so idle and decadent that they began to lose the will to defend their class interests.

It was the growth of selfishness and individual gratification among the Roman elite that Morris claimed was responsible for the collapse of ancient civilization. Whereas the early valour of the Roman legions had gained his grudging respect, he considered the corruption of these values by the pursuit of wealth to have led to the complete destruction of public spirit. The Roman soldier—once a citizen religiously devoted to his city—soon became a bribed hireling. Ultimately no bribe was high enough to induce a civilized man to fight, with the result

that the Roman legions were manned by the very barbarians
whose kinsmen were attacking the Empire from without. Thus
the Roman Empire fell as a result of its own internal contradictions and its inability to defend itself against the incursions of the
Germanic tribes of the north and east.

Morris was attracted to this early period of human civilization
for a number of reasons which were closely linked to his socialist
propaganda campaign. The first of these was his belief that an
historical affinity of sorts could be traced between modern
English people and the early Germanic peoples. This idea was
almost certainly derived in part, as Amanda Hodgson has
suggested, from his reading of British historians such as Elton,
Freeman, Green and Stubbs, all of whom considered it possible
to trace the origins of contemporary social and political institutions to the practices of the early Teutonic people. As Stubbs
wrote, 'The English are not aboriginal [but] ... are a people of
German descent in the main constituents of blood, character, and
language.'[10] He went on to add that they were also the inheritors
'of the elements of primitive German civilization and the
common germs of German institutions'.[11]

In fact Morris's view of the organic link between the early
Germanic tribes and modern English people is less straight-
forward than Hodgson suggests. In 'Early England', a lecture
which traced the history of England from the time of the Roman
invasion to the Norman Conquest, he argued that these two
events had partially severed the association. At the time of the
Roman conquest he claimed that the indigenous English
population had still barely progressed beyond the stage of
savagery and were only just 'tending towards a tribal condition'
(p. 53). These indigenous potentialities were destroyed by the
arrival of the Romans with their 'civilized' ideas. A second
opportunity for the Teutonic peoples occurred when the Romans
were in turn replaced by the tribes of the English, the Jutes, and
the Saxons whom Morris regarded as the direct descendants of

the German tribes who had originated in 'the great forests of mid-Europe' (p. 58). At the time of their invasion of England these tribesmen were, significantly, 'at the point of federating if they had not already federated into a bigger body "the people"' (p. 56).

Even so Morris believed England would have remained a Germanic nation if it had not been for the Norman Conquest. It was this infiltration of Norman blood and culture—referred to contemptuously in 'Feudal England' as having 'developed from Roman provincials'—which Morris believed had prevented the English from becoming a 'great homogenous Teutonic people infused usefully with a mixture of Celtic blood' (p. 73). For this reason, while he exploited the perceived link between the Goths and modern English people for propaganda purposes, he always did so in order to emphasize the corruption of these ancient ideas under conditions of modern capitalism. Whereas the English historians of the 1870s and 1880s saw tribal practices as the foundation on which modern institutions had evolved and improved, Morris used them to show how such institutions reflect the health of the society from which they originated. This argument was a logical extension of a line of thought already apparent in his pre-socialist lectures. If artistic creation mirrored the social environment in which it was produced, then it followed that social institutions would do so too.

In 'The Development of Modern Society' Morris maintained that although contemporary society superficially retained some tribal institutions in modified form, these cultural remnants were merely travesties of the spirit of the originals. To prove the point he used the example of the 'moot' which some nineteenth-century historians had cited as the origin of modern judicial arrangements. In the case of the 'moot' Morris cited two funda-mental differences in conditions pertaining under barbarism which made it completely inappropriate to compare it with similar judicial arrangements under capitalism. The first was that under barbarism all the duties of a freeman had reference to the community in which he lived. His personal interests were therefore synonymous with those of his tribe which meant that 'the assertion of any ... private interests would have been looked upon as a crime, or rather a monstrosity, hardly possible to understand' (p. 109). Thus under barbarism the administration of justice reflected the will of the whole people rather than serving as an instrument of class oppression as it did under capitalism. Morris's second point was that the popular nineteenth-century democratic concept of 'government by the majority' was meaningless under a tribal system. As individuals derived their very existence from their integration into the tribe it was inconceivable that given this strong bond anyone could assert an opinion prejudicial to the interests of the community as a whole.

Morris was also attracted to the life of the tribes as their social practices provided ideal models from which to derive a vision of the organization of post-capitalist society. In the late 1880s Morris spent some time seeking to establish 'vision' as a legitimate socialist propaganda technique. He argued that such a vision should be derived from a synthesis of historical realism with imaginative insights emanating from the author's own 'instinct'. Barbarism provided an ideal starting point for such a 'vision' as it was based on concepts such as community, freedom, equality and common ownership all of which could be assumed to play an important role in a future communist state. As Morris put it in a letter to Georgiana Burne-Jones in May 1885, 'how often it consoles me to think of barbarism once more flooding the world, and real feelings and passions, however rudimentary, taking the place of our wretched hypocrisies'.[12] Coincidentally, Engels made precisely the same point at the end of *The Origins of the Family* when he quoted a passage from Morgan's *Ancient Society* in which the latter, speculating on the next stage of human history, had written, [Engels' italics] *'It will be a revival, in a higher form of liberty, equality and fraternity of the ancient gens'.*[13]

It was probably for this reason that Morris decided to dramatize the lives of the Teutonic tribes in two prose romances he wrote in the late 1880s. The first of these, *The House of the Wolfings* (1888), was set during the period of barbarism in which the individual gens were assimilated into the wider concept of the tribe. This was followed a year later by *The Roots of the Mountains* which explored the next stage in the progressive development of barbarism: that of the gradual association of the tribes into a people. There is some evidence that Morris planned a third volume in this series. A tantalizing fragment of another prose romance has survived, entitled *The Story of Desiderius*, which is set in one of the southern cities in Italy—possibly Verona—during the final days of the Roman Empire. In what remains of the text the hero, Desiderius, falls in love with his mother's new slave who has just been captured from the Goths. Although Morris abandoned the tale shortly after describing this episode, it is probable that he would have gone on to detail the barbarians final clash with the declining Empire and the complex social and psychological implications this would have had for the two lovers divided by an insurmountable cultural gulf.

Morris considered the rise of feudalism in Europe following the collapse of the Roman Empire to have been related to the Teutonic and Gothic tribes' success in side-stepping the stage of city life. This had two consequences. First, it meant that the development of their customs had remained relatively unaffected through time and 'differed little from each other, and not much from those of the classical peoples before their development of the city and its life' (p. 115). Secondly, it meant that when they succeeded in overthrowing the Roman Empire the new 'feudal system was based not on the city and its wards, urban and rural, as was the case in ancient society, but on the country district, the manor and its townships' (p. 116). In 'The Development of Modern Society' he described this process in a specifically British context:

When our Anglo-Saxon forefathers first conquered Romanised
Britain, they did not know what to do with the cities they won; they
let them lie in ruins, and went to live down the dales on the borders
of the streams in their homelands, just as their ancestors had done in
the clearings of the great central forest of Europe (p. 116).

Morris identified two stages in the subsequent development
of feudal society—the second great epoch in human history—
which he argued were linked by a transitional phase that took
place in the second half of the fourteenth century. The first stage
was one in which, to a lesser or greater extent, social relations
were based on a theoretical model of feudal rights and obligations. This model he characterized as one 'of an unbroken chain
of service from the serf up to the emperor, and of protection
from the emperor down to the serf' (p. 148). It recognized no
absolute ownership of the land as God was considered the one
owner of the earth. His authority was simply vested in the king
and his nobles who were empowered to devolve this authority to
their feudal vassals and ultimately the serf on whose labour the
whole hierarchy lived. The serf had no rights except that of
protection by his lord from those outside the manor in which he
lived. For the serf his personal lord 'was the incarnation of the
compulsion and protection of God' (p. 148-9).

This feudal hierarchy was only possible because of the type of
religion that prevailed at the time. What distinguished the early
Middle Ages from classical times was that the individualistic
devotion encouraged by early Christianity had evolved into a
genuine fellowship of the Church. The old idea that the Church
should exist in isolation from the State gave way to the view that
its should participate in both temporal and spiritual matters in
order to foster and encourage heavenly virtues. The Church not
only acted as the link between the earthly and heavenly
kingdoms, but also sought to influence people to adopt the values
of equality, fraternity and fellowship in their temporal affairs. As
Morris put it in *Socialism from the Root Up*, the task of the Church

was to bring 'the kingdom of heaven to earth by breathing its spirit into the temporal power' (p. 149).

Despite the laudable sentiments of the theory—and some notable achievements in the fields of architecture and the handicrafts—Morris argued that by 1350 the structure of early medieval society had already begun to be undermined. The main reason for this was that in most countries feudalism had not existed in its purest form. In *Socialism from the Root Up* he claimed that it only reached its fullest expression in the medieval German empire. Elsewhere it only existed in an imperfect form. In England, for example, he argued that 'the monarchy soon gained complete predominance over the great barons, and a kind of bureaucracy soon sprang up which interfered with the full working of the feudal system' (p. 148). By thus concentrating power in the hands of a few it was not long before the more unscrupulous had sought to abuse their privileged position for personal gain. When these abuses occurred they were often met with open rebellion amongst the serfs. As examples of these protests Morris cited the activities of Robin Hood in England and the Jacquerie in France. Although these uprisings never threatened the stability of feudal society they did have a psychological significance in encouraging ordinary people to develop an independence of mind and a desire for personal liberty.

Morris argued that after 1350 feudalism was further destabilized by the rise of the guilds. He claimed that these had originated in the vestiges of ideas which had survived from the primitive communism of the tribes. At first the guilds existed as benefit societies which operated within the existing framework of feudalism. Morris described their role in 'The Development of Modern Society' as redeeming 'their members from captivity; to set them up in business again if they were ruined; [and] to pay their fines if they came into the clutch of the law' (p. 119). From these early guilds evolved the guilds-merchant which were associations for the protection of trade. The crucial development, however, occurred in the fourteenth-century when the guilds-merchant were in turn transformed. They were either assimilated into the existing corporations of the free towns or radically reconstituted into new craft-guilds with the aim of protecting and regulating the handicrafts. In *Socialism from the Root Up* Morris claimed that this tendency to association was bitterly opposed by both the Church and State. However, in the long run it could not be resisted and the craft-guilds were eventually accepted as part of the feudal system.

The rise of the craft-guilds was accompanied by changes in the ancient conditions of serfdom. Many of the field serfs began to drift to the towns where they were obliged, in order to obtain work, to become affiliated to the craft-guilds as journeymen. This meant that the workshops no longer consisted of the master and his apprentices but also a number of inferior workmen thus laying the foundations of the future class-based society. At the same time another group of serfs was able to escape their ancient feudal obligations and assume the status of 'free labourers'. This group was subsequently to become the copyholding class, farming land whose tenure remained unfree.

Morris considered one of the crucial events in the break-up of serfdom in England to have been the Peasant's Revolt of 1381. This he regarded as one of the first examples of the people being mobilized for a serious political purpose. In 'The Lord Mayor's Show', an article published in *Justice* on 15 November 1884, he wrote, 'we need make no mistake about the cause for which Wat Tyler and his worthier associate John Ball fell; they were fighting against the fleecing then in fashion, viz.; serfdom or villeinage, which was already beginning to wane before the advance of the industrial gild' (p. 136). For the people the rebellion was about personal freedom and economic independence. They aspired to nothing less than the abolition of the feudal obligations that bound them to their masters. Morris later dramatized the events surrounding the Peasant's Revolt in his prose romance, *A Dream of John Ball*, which was serialized in *Commonweal* in 1886-87.

The break-up of serfdom was one of the factors that contributed to the rise of commerce (the precursor of capitalism). According to Morris medieval society 'knew nothing of capitalistic exchange: the demands of the local markets were supplied by the direct exchange of the superfluity of the produce of the various districts and countries' (p. 153). In *Socialism from the Root Up* he argued that this began to change in the fifteenth and sixteenth centuries with the development of a world market in which all commodities were sold for money. This in turn led to the creation of what he termed 'a huckstering class' who carried on this new trade. This class soon began to gain economic power at a time when the old feudal society, with its duly ordered grades, was in the process of disintegration.

In England the demands of this new commerce led to changes in agricultural production. The landlords soon recognized that the old tillage system of the manor was an inefficient use of the country's rich pastoral land. They realized that their profits could be greatly increased if the old yeomen's holdings could be abolished and their land turned over to pasture. In order to profit from the demand for English wool the landlords therefore rack-rented their tenants, expropriated the yeomen and drove more of the labourers off the land to work as 'free' journeymen in the towns.

This rise of commercialism was accompanied by the gradual severance of the feudal link between the spiritual and temporal powers. The individualistic ethics of Early Christianity, which had been submerged under feudalism, re-emerged and began to replace 'the corporate ethics' prevalent in medieval Catholicism. This revived Christianity took hold of the most progressive minds of the period 'so that Protestantism became the real religion of the epoch' (p. 156). According to Morris the Protestant religion was as essential to the success of commercialism as

medieval Catholicism had been to feudalism. As he and Bax
wrote in *Socialism from the Root Up*,

> everywhere the new religion became the useful servant of commer-
> cialism, first by providing a new army of officials always subservient
> to the authority of government, and secondly by holding out to the
> people hopes outside their wretched life on earth, so as to quiet their
> discontent by turning their earthly aspirations heavenward (p. 156).

In effect 'the Church was extinct; it was a mere salaried adjunct
of the State' (pp. 156-7).

Morris claimed that in England feudalism gave way to
commercialism in the late sixteenth and early seventeenth
centuries. As with previous economic changes this development
was accompanied by great misery amongst the working people.
The expropriation of the yeomanry from the land and the conversion of tillage into pasture created a vast body of unemployed
free men who had little prospect of finding work in an economy
that was still primarily based on agriculture. Serious social unrest
was only avoided when in Elizabethan times a Poor Law was
passed that Morris described as 'far more humane than might
have been expected from the way in which the poor had been
dealt with up to that time' (p. 160). In the early seventeenth
century this process was also aided by the growth of the towns
which stimulated agriculture and led to a revival of tillage. As a
result Morris claimed that from the middle of the seventeenth
century England entered a period of reasonable prosperity.

In common with Marx and Engels, Morris believed that
England was well in advance of its continental neighbours in the
movement from feudalism to capitalism. He and Bax argued in
Socialism from the Root Up that on the continent the old feudal
practices took much longer to break down. Part of the reason for
this was that in countries like France and Germany the peasants
suffered far greater oppression than those in England as 'the gilds
had still some life and power, and the people were not utterly
divorced from the land as in England' (p. 161). They were also

further 'crushed by the frightful wars which passed over them—
in all which religion was the immediate cause': that is, struggles
in one form or another between Catholics and Protestants
(p. 161). Amongst these conflicts he and Bax cited that in
Holland against the Spanish, the 'Thirty Years' War' in Germany
and the Massacre of St Bartholomew in France.

Morris identified two stages in the subsequent development
of capitalism in England. The first he referred to as that characterized by 'the division of labour system'. In the late seventeenth
and eighteenth centuries the world markets began to expand
enormously and it soon became apparent that demand could no
longer be satisfied by traditional methods of production. In order
to increase production the division of labour system was adopted
in the old craft workshops. Morris and Bax described the basis of
this system in *Socialism from the Root Up* as one in which

> the unit of labour is not an individual man, but a group, every
> member of which is helpless by himself, but trained by constant
> practice to the repetition of a small part of the work, acquires great
> precision and speed in its performance. In short each man is not so
> much a machine as a part of a machine (p. 170).

Under this system the worker was divorced from the object of
his labour and no longer had any specific craft skill. This made
him entirely dependent on his master for employment. His only
hope of opposing his employer was to combine with his fellow
workers thus providing the first indications of the class struggle
that Morris believed would ultimately bring down the whole
capitalist system.

The division of labour system supplied the demands of the
world market until the end of the eighteenth century. It was then
superseded by the growth of the great machine industries during
the Industrial Revolution. With the rise of this new manufacturing industry the conditions of labour underwent yet another
change. As Morris wrote in 'The Hopes of Civilization',

> industrial productiveness was increased prodigiously, but so far from
> the workers reaping the benefit of this, they were thrown out of work
> in enormous numbers, while those who were still employed were
> reduced from the position of skilled artisans to that of unskilled
> labourers (p. 38).

The sudden industrial change was as usual accompanied by
considerable social unrest. As examples of this Morris cited the
outbreak of Ludditism and the 'Swing' and 'Plug' riots.

Morris considered the most scandalous consequence of the
Industrial Revolution to have been the blatant exploitation of
ordinary working men and women. As he and Bax wrote in
Socialism from the Root Up,

> in the earlier period of this industrial revolution the change was
> tremendous and sudden and the sufferings of the working classes
> very great, as no attempt was made to alleviate the distress that was
> sure to be caused by the change from the use of human hands to
> machinery (p. 171).

This distress was most obvious in the North of England
where the manufacturers' ruthless pursuit of profit led them to
employ women and children in the place of men. So dreadful
were the results of this practice that the government was
eventually forced to alleviate the worst excesses by passing a
series of Factory Acts. Morris made it clear, however, that these
reforms were passed to defend the system and 'were not
intended to benefit the great mass of adult workers, but rather
concessions to the outcry of the philanthropists at the condition
of the women and especially the children so employed' (p. 173).

It was following the passing of the Factory Acts that Morris
argued that the class struggle began to take a more organized
form. The first indication of this was the rise of trade unionism
amongst the skilled workers in the early part of the nineteenth
century. At first these trade unions acted as benefit societies in
much the same way as the craft-guilds had done in the early
Middle Ages. However, as time passed they found themselves

forced—as the craft-guilds had done—to 'take in hand matters dealing with the regulation of labour' (p. 173).

In *Socialism from the Root Up* Morris and Bax identified two phases in the history of capitalism in England during the second half of the nineteenth century. The first was its prosperous period. This they dated from the abolition of the Corn Laws in 1847 which had led to a reduction in food prices and increased the standard of living of the workers. Other beneficial factors that contributed to the success of capitalism during this period they identified as the discovery of gold in California and Australia, the prodigious increase in the luxury and expenditure of the upper and middle classes and the gradual perfection of the great machine industries. All these developments, they argued, had combined to give at least the appearance of general prosperity in the country during the mid-Victorian period.

Morris and Bax dated the first signs of the decline of the capitalistic system in England to the early 1880s. At this time a combination of ever more severe trade depressions and increased competition in the world market from countries like Germany and America had led to a fall in exports and high unemployment. This tended to support their view, derived in part from Marx's *Das Kapital*, that capitalism was doomed by its own innate contradictions. As they wrote in *Socialism from the Root Up*,

> the commerce of the great industries has entered insensibly into its second stage, and mere cut-throat competition between the different nations has taken the place of the benevolent commercial despotism of the only nation which was thoroughly prepared to take advantage of the Industrial Revolution—Great Britain, to wit.
>
> The second stage is doubtless preparing the final one which will end with the death of the whole bourgeois commercial system (p. 175).

They went on to predict that this economic disintegration would lead to an increasing gulf between the bourgeoisie and the proletariat and be accompanied by the rise of class consciousness. Therein lay the potential for the next great revolutionary change:

the break up of the system which has created [the proletariat] ... shall *force* them into a revolt against it. In the course of that revolt this great middle-class will in its turn be absorbed into the proletariat, which will form a new Society, in which classes will have ceased to exist. This is the next Revolution, as inevitable, as inexorable as the rising of to-morrow's sun (p. 176).

With hindsight Morris's anticipation of the imminence of social revolution seems incredibly optimistic. Over a century has passed since he wrote these words yet capitalism remains the predominant form of economic organization throughout the developed world. Even the former 'communist' states of Eastern Europe have abandoned their command economies in favour of the workings of the 'free' market. Nor does Morris's sophisticated analysis of human history lend much support to the view that profound economic and social change can be accomplished by sudden revolutionary acts. Those historical events he singled out for special attention—such as the Peasant's Revolt and the Paris Commune—were symbols, rather than agents, of social change. As Morris's historical writings demonstrate so well the history of human society has been evolutionary not cataclysmic.

However, this is to miss the central propaganda purpose of Morris's historical writings. At the beginning of *Socialism from the Root Up* he and Bax claimed that the study of history gave socialists both an 'encouragement and [a] warning which we cannot afford to disregard' (p. 144). The warning was for those who sought to defend capitalism by ignoring the evolutionary nature of human history and presenting their system as permanent and unchangeable. For Morris and Bax such a position was untenable as it ignored the inevitability of historical change: 'Our opponents ... are trying consciously to stay that very evolution at the point which it has reached today; they are attempting to turn the transient into the eternal; therefore, for them history has no lessons' (p. 144). The socialists, on the other hand, accepted that human history was characterized by change. No form of social organization had ever proved to be permanent.

Barbarism had melted into feudalism as inevitably as feudalism had into capitalism. It was the socialists' role to recognize the next change 'to clear away obstacles to it, to accept it, and to be ready to organise it in detail' (p. 144). Ultimately, the lesson of history for Morris was not what it taught us about the past but what it promised us for the future.

Notes

1. E. LeMire (ed.), *The Unpublished Lectures of William Morris* (Detroit: Wayne State University Press, 1969), pp. 301, 302, 304, 308 and 312.

2. 'The Development of Modern Society' was serialized in *Commonweal* between 19 July and 16 August 1890.

3. E.P. Thompson, *William Morris: Romantic to Revolutionary* (New York: Pantheon, 1977), p. 28.

4. Thompson, *William Morris*, p. 28.

5. M. Morris (ed.), *The Collected Works of William Morris* (London: Longman, Green & Co, 1910-15), XIV, p. xxv.

6. A. Hodgson, *The Romances of William Morris* (London: Cambridge University Press, 1987), pp. 134-36.

7. J. Goode, 'William Morris and the Dream of Revolution', in J. Lucas (ed.), *Literature and Politics in the Nineteenth Century* (London: Methuen & Co, 1971), pp. 261-65.

8. Morris (ed.), *The Collected Works*, XXII, p. 319.

9. LeMire (ed.), *The Unpublished Lectures*, p. 99.

10. W. Stubbs, *The Constitutional History of England in its Origins and Development* (London, 1874-78), I, p. 2.

11. Stubbs, *Constitutional History*, p. 2.

12. N. Kelvin (ed.), *The Collected Letters of William Morris* (Princeton: Princeton University Press, 1987), II, p. 436.

13. *Karl Marx and Frederick Engels: Selected Writings* (London: Lawrence & Wishart, 1968), p. 583. The original quote appeared in L.H. Morgan, *Ancient Society, or Researches in the Line of Human Progress from Savagery through Barbarism to Civilisation* (London: Macmillan & Co, 1877), p. 552.

NOTES ON TEXTS

The Hopes of Civilization, 1885

This lecture was first delivered by Morris on 14 June 1885 at a meeting sponsored by the Hammersmith branch of the Socialist League at Kelmscott House, Hammersmith. The text is taken from *The Collected Works of William Morris*, XXIII, pp. 59-80.

Early England, 1886

This lecture was first delivered by Morris on 12 December 1886 at a meeting sponsored by the Hammersmith branch of the Socialist League at Kelmscott House, Hammersmith. It was the first in a trilogy of lectures on 'England, As It Was, As It Is, and As It May Be'. The lecture was first published in Eugene LeMire's book *The Unpublished Lectures of William Morris*, pp. 158-179. I would like to thank the Society of Antiquaries for giving me their written permission to reprint the lecture in the present volume.

Feudal England, 1887

This lecture was first delivered by Morris at a meeting on 13 February 1887 sponsored by the Hammersmith branch of the Socialist League at Kelmscott House, Hammersmith. The text is taken from *Commonweal* where it was serialized between 20 August 1887 and 10 September 1887. This version has some minor variations from that published in *The Collected Works of William Morris*, XXIII, pp. 39-58. The lecture was the second in the trilogy 'England, As it Was, As It Is, and As It May Be'.

Art and Industry in the Fourteenth Century, 1887

This lecture was first delivered by Morris at a meeting on 15 May 1887 sponsored by the Hammersmith branch of the Socialist League at Kelmscott House, Hammersmith. The text is taken from *The Collected Works of William Morris*, XXII, pp. 375-390. Eugene LeMire has pointed out that published versions of this lecture differ from the manuscript version preserved as B.M.Add.MS.45331(9). This was the final lecture in the trilogy 'England, As It Was, As It Is, and As It May Be'.

The Development of Modern Society, 1890

This lecture was first delivered by Morris at a meeting on 13 April 1890 sponsored by the Liverpool Socialist Society at the Rodney Hall, Liverpool. The text is taken from *Commonweal* where it was serialized between 19 July 1890 and 16 August 1890.

The Lord Mayor's Show, 1884

The text of this article first appeared in *Justice*, Volume I, Number 44, 15 November 1884, p. 2.

Why We Celebrate The Commune of Paris, 1887

The text of this article first appeared in *Commonweal*, Volume 3, Number 62, 19 May 1887, pp. 89-90.

Revolutionary Calendar: Wat Tyler, 1888

The text of this article first appeared in *Commonweal*, Volume 4, Number 126, 9 June 1888, p. 182.

Socialism from the Root Up, 1886

The chapters from *Socialism from the Root Up* first appeared in serialized form in *Commonweal* between 15 May 1886 and 14 August 1886. They were later revised and published in book form as part of *Socialism: Its Growth and Outcome* (London: Swan Sonnenschein 1893).

LECTURES

THE HOPES OF CIVILIZATION

1885

Every age has had its hopes, hopes that look to something beyond the life of the age itself, hopes that try to pierce into the future; and, strange to say, I believe that those hopes have been stronger not in the heyday of the epoch which has given them birth, but rather in its decadence and times of corruption: in sober truth it may well be that these hopes are but a reflection in those that live happily and comfortably of the vain longings of those others who suffer with little power of expressing their sufferings in an audible voice: when all goes well the happy world forgets these people and their desires, sure as it is that their woes are not dangerous to them the wealthy: whereas when the woes and grief of the poor begin to rise to a point beyond the endurance of men, fear conscious or unconscious falls upon the rich, and they begin to look about them to see what there may be among the elements of their society which may be used as palliatives for the misery which, long existing and ever growing greater among the slaves of that society, is now at last forcing itself on the attention of the masters. Times of change, disruption, and revolution are naturally times of hope also, and not seldom the hopes of something better to come are the first tokens that tell people that revolution is at hand, though commonly such tokens are no more believed than Cassandra's prophecies, or are even taken in a contrary sense by those who have anything to lose; since they look upon them as signs of the prosperity of the times, and the long endurance of that state of things which is so kind to them. Let us then see what the hopes of civilization are like to-day: for indeed I purpose speaking of our own times chiefly, and will leave for the present all mention of that older civilization which was destroyed by the healthy barbarism out of which our present society has grown.

Yet a few words may be necessary concerning the birth of our present epoch and the hopes it gave rise to, and what has become of them: that will not take us very far back in history; as to my mind our modern civilization begins with the stirring period about the time of the Reformation in England, the time which in the then more important countries of the Continent is know as the period of the Renaissance, the so-called new birth of art and learning.

And first remember that this period includes the death-throes of feudalism, with all the good and evil which that system bore with it. For centuries past its end was getting ready by the gradual weakening of the bonds of the great hierarchy which held men together: the characteristics of those bonds were, theoretically at least, personal rights and personal duties between superior and inferior all down the scale; each man was born, so to say, subject to these conditions, and the mere accidents of his life could not free him from them: commerce, in our sense of the word, there was none; capitalistic manufacture, capitalistic exchange was unknown: to buy goods cheap that you might sell them dear was a legal offence (forestalling): to buy goods in the market in the morning and to sell them in the afternoon in the same place was not thought a useful occupation and was forbidden under the name of regrating; usury, instead of leading as now directly to the highest offices of the State, was thought wrong, and the profit of it mostly fell to the chosen people of God: the robbery of the workers, thought necessary then as now to the very existence of the State, was carried out quite crudely without any concealment or excuse by arbitrary taxation or open violence: on the other hand, life was easy, and common necessaries plenteous; the holidays of the Church were holidays in the modern sense of the word, down-right play-days, and there were ninety-six obligatory ones: nor were the people tame and sheep-like, but as rough-handed and bold a set of good fellows as ever rubbed through life under the sun.

I remember three passages, from contemporary history or gossip, about the life of those times which luck has left us, and which illustrate curiously the change that has taken place in the habits of Englishmen. A lady writing from Norfolk 400 years ago to her husband in London, amidst various commissions for tapestries, groceries, and gowns, bids him also not to forget to bring back with him a good supply of cross-bows and bolts, since the windows of their hall were too low to be handy for long-bow shooting. A German traveller, writing quite at the end of the mediæval period, speaks of the English as the laziest and proudest people and the best cooks in Europe. A Spanish ambassador about the same period says, "These English live in houses built of sticks and mud,* but therein they fare as plenteously as lords."

Indeed, I confess that it is with a strange emotion that I recall these times and try to realize the life of our forefathers, men who were named like ourselves, spoke nearly the same tongue, lived on the same spots of earth, and therewithal were as different from us in manners, habits, ways of life and thought, as though they lived in another planet. The very face of the country has changed; not merely I mean in London and the great manufacturing centres, but through the country generally; there is no piece of English ground, except such places as Salisbury Plain, but bears witness to the amazing change which 400 years has brought upon us.

Not seldom I please myself with trying to realize the face of mediæval England; the many chases and great woods, the stretches of common tillage and common pasture quite unenclosed; the rough husbandry of the tilled parts, the

unimproved breeds of cattle, sheep, and swine; especially the
latter, so lank and long and lathy, looking so strange to us; the
strings of packhorses along the bridle-roads, the scantiness of the
wheel-roads, scarce any except those left by the Romans, and
those made from monastery to monastery: the scarcity of bridges,
and people using ferries instead, or fords where they could; the
little towns, well bechurched, often walled; the villages just
where they are now (except for those that have nothing but the
church left to tell of them), but better and more populous; their
churches, some big and handsome, some small and curious, but
all crowded with altars and furniture, and gay with pictures and
ornament; the many religious houses, with their glorious architecture; the beautiful manor-houses, some of them castles once,
and survivals from an earlier period; some new and elegant; some
out of all proportion small for the importance of their lords.
How strange it would be to us if we could be landed in
fourteenth century England! Unless we saw the crest of some
familiar hill, like that which yet bears upon it a symbol of an
English tribe, and from which, looking down on the plain where
Alfred was born, I once had many such ponderings, we should
not know into what country of the world we were come: the
name is left, scarce a thing else.

And when I think of this it quickens my hope of what may be:
even so it will be with us in time to come; all will have changed,
and another people will be dwelling here in England, who,
although they may be of our blood and bear our name, will
wonder how we lived in the nineteenth century.

Well, under all that rigidly ordered caste society of the fourteenth century, with its rough plenty, its sauntering life, its cool
acceptance of rudeness and violence, there was going on a keen
struggle of classes which carried with it the hope of progress
of those days: the serfs gradually getting freed, and becoming
some of them the town population, the first journeymen, or
"free labourers," so called, some of them the copyholders of

agricultural land: the corporations of the towns gathered power, the craft-gilds grew into perfection and corruption, the power of the Crown increased, attended with nascent bureaucracy; in short, the middle class was forming underneath the outward show of feudalism still intact: and all was getting ready for the beginning of the great commercial epoch in whose *latter* days I would fain hope we are living. That epoch began with the portentous change of agriculture which meant cultivating for profit instead of for livelihood, and which carried with it the expropriation of the *people* from the land, the extinction of the yeoman, and the rise of the capitalist farmer; and the growth of the town population, which, swelled by the drift of the landless vagabonds and masterless men, grew into a definite proletariat or class of free-workmen; and their existence made that of the embryo capitalist-manufacturer also possible; and the reign of commercial contract and cash payment began to take the place of the old feudal hierarchy, with its many-linked chain of personal responsibilities. The latter half of the seventeenth century, the reign of Charles II, saw the last blow struck at this feudal system, when the landowners' military service was abolished, and they became simple owners of property that had no duties attached to it save the payment of a land-tax.

The hopes of the early part of the commercial period may be read in almost every book of the time, expressed in various degrees of dull or amusing pedantry, and show a naïf arrogance and contempt of the times just past through which nothing but the utmost simplicity of ignorance could have attained to. But the times were stirring, and gave birth to the most powerful individualities in many branches of literature, and More and Campanella, at least from the midst of the exuberant hopes of times yet to come when that commercialism itself should have given place to the society which we hope will be the next transform[ation] of civilization into something else: into a new social life.

This period of early and exuberant hopes passed into the next stage of sober realization of many of them, for commerce grew and grew, and moulded all society to its needs: the workman of the sixteenth century worked still as an individual with little co-operation, and scarce any division of labour: by the end of the seventeenth he had become only a part of a group which by that time was in the handicrafts the real unit of production; division of labour even at that period had quite destroyed his individuality, and the worker was but part of a machine: all through the eighteenth century this system went on progressing towards perfection, till to most men of that period, to most of those who were in any way capable of expressing their thoughts, civilization had already reached a high stage of perfection, and was certain to go on from better to better.

These hopes were not on the surface of a very revolutionary kind, but nevertheless the class struggle still went on, and quite openly too; for the remains of feudality, aided by the mere mask and grimace of the religion which was once a real part of the feudal system, hampered the progress of commerce sorely, and seemed a thousandfold more powerful than it really was; because in spite of the class struggle there was really a covert alliance between the powerful middle classes who were the children of commerce and their old masters the aristocracy; an unconscious understanding between them rather, in the midst of their contest, that certain matters were to be respected even by the advanced party. The contest and civil war between the king and the commons in England in the seventeenth century illustrate[s] this well: the caution with which privilege was attacked in the beginning of the struggle, the unwillingness of all the leaders save a few enthusiasts to carry matters to their logical consequences, even when the march of events had developed the antagonism between aristocratic privilege and middle-class freedom of contract (so called); finally, the crystallization of the new order conquered by the sword of Naseby into a mongrel

condition of things between privilege and bourgeois freedom, the
defeat and grief of the purist Republicans, and the horror at and
swift extinction of the Levellers, the pioneers of Socialism in that
day, all point to the fact that the "party of progress," as we should
call it now, was determined after all that privilege should not be
abolished further than its own standpoint.

The seventeenth century ended in the great Whig revolution
in England, and, as I said, commerce throve and grew enormously, and the power of the middle classes increased proportionately
and all things seemed going smoothly with them, till at last in
France the culminating corruption of a society still nominally
existing for the benefit of the privileged aristocracy, forced their
hand: the old order of things, backed as it was by the power of
the executive, by that semblance of overwhelming physical force
which is the real and only cement of a society founded on the
slavery of the many—the aristocracy power—seemed strong and
almost inexpugnable: and since any stick will do to beat a dog
with, the middle classes in France were forced to take up the first
stick that lay ready to hand if they were not to give way to the
aristocrats, which indeed the whole evolution of history forbade
them to do. Therefore, as in England in the seventeenth century,
the middle classes allied themselves to religious and republican,
and even communistic enthusiasts, with the intention, firm
though unexpressed, to keep them down when they had
mounted to power by their means, so in France they had to ally
themselves with the proletariat; which, shamefully oppressed and
degraded as it had been, now for the first time in history began
to feel its power, the power of numbers: by means of this help
they triumphed over aristocratic privilege, but, on the other
hand, although the proletariat was speedily reduced again to a
position not much better than that it had held before the
revolution, the part it played therein gave a new and terrible
character to that revolution, and from that time forward the class
struggle entered on to a new phase; the middle classes had gained

a complete victory, which in France carried with it all the outward signs of victory, though in England they chose to consider a certain part of themselves an aristocracy, who had indeed little signs of aristocracy about them either for good or for evil, being in very few cases of long descent, and being in their manners and ideas unmistakably *bourgeois*.

So was accomplished the second act of the great class struggle with whose first act began the age of commerce; as to the hopes of this period of the revolution we all know how extravagant they were; what a complete regeneration of the world was expected to result from the abolition of the grossest form of privilege; and I must say that, before we mock at the extravagance of those hopes, we should try to put ourselves in the place of those that held them, and try to conceive how the privilege of the old noblesse must have galled the respectable well-to-do people of that time. Well, the reasonable part of those hopes were realized by the revolution; in other words, it accomplished what it really aimed at, the freeing of commerce from the fetters of sham feudality; or, in other words, the destruction of aristocratic privilege. The more extravagant part of the hopes expressed by the eighteenth century revolution were vague enough, and tended in the direction of supposing that the working classes would be benefited by what was to the interest of the middle class in some way quite unexplained—by a kind of magic, one may say—which welfare of the workers, as it was never directly aimed at, but only hoped for by the way, so also did not come about by any such magical means, and the triumphant middle classes began gradually to find themselves looked upon no longer as rebellious servants, but as oppressive masters.

The middle class had freed commerce from her fetters of privilege, and had freed thought from her fetters of theology, at least partially; but it had not freed, nor attempted to free, labour from its fetters. The leaders of the French Revolution, even amidst the fears, suspicions, and slaughter of the Terror, upheld

the rights of "property" so called, though a new pioneer or
prophet appeared in France, analogous in some respects to the
Levellers of Cromwell's time, but, as might be expected, far more
advanced and reasonable than they were. Gracchus Babeuf and
his fellows were treated as criminals, and died or suffered the
torture of prison for attempting to put into practice those words
which the Republic still carried on its banners, and Liberty,
Fraternity, and Equality were interpreted in a middle-class, or if
you please a Jesuitical, sense, as the rewards of success for those
who could struggle into an exclusive class; and at last property
had to be defended by a military adventurer, and the Revolution
seemed to have ended with Napoleonism.

Nevertheless, the Revolution was not dead, nor was it
possible to say thus far and no further to the rising tide.
Commerce, which had created the propertyless proletariat
throughout civilization, had still another part to play, which is
not yet played out; she had and has to teach the workers to know
what they are; to educate them, to consolidate them, and not
only to give them aspirations for their advancement as a class, but
to make means for them to realize those aspirations. All this she
did, nor loitered in her work either; from the beginning of the
nineteenth century the history of civilisation is really the history
of the last of the class-struggles which was inaugurated by the
French Revolution; and England, who all through the times of
the Revolution and the Cæsarism which followed it appeared to
be the steady foe of Revolution, was really as steadily furthering
it; her natural conditions, her store of coal and minerals, her
temperate climate, extensive sea-board and many harbours, and
lastly her position as the outpost of Europe looking into America
across the ocean, doomed her to be for a time at least the mistress
of the commerce of the civilized world, and its agent with
barbarous and semi-barbarous countries. The necessities of this
destiny drove her into the implacable war with France, a war
which, nominally waged on behalf of monarchical principles, was

really, though doubtless unconsciously, carried on for the possession of the foreign and colonial markets. She came out victorious from that war, and fully prepared to take advantage of the industrial revolution which had been going on the while, and which I now ask you to note.

I have said that the eighteenth century perfected the system of labour which took the place of the mediæval system, under which a workman individually carried his piece of work all through its various stages from the first to the last.

This new system, the first change in industrial production since the Middle Ages, is known as the system of division of labour, wherein, as I said, the unit of labour is a group, not a man; the individual workman in this system is kept life-long at the performance of some task quite petty in itself, and which he soon masters, and having mastered it has nothing more to do but to go on increasing his speed of hand under the spur of competition with his fellows, until he has become the perfect machine which it is his ultimate duty to become, since without attaining to that end he must die or become a pauper. You can well imagine how this glorious invention of division of labour, this complete destruction of individuality in the workman, and his apparent hopeless enslavement to his profit-grinding master, stimulated the hopes of civilization; probably more hymns have been sung in praise of division of labour, more sermons preached about it, than have done homage to the precept, "do unto others as ye would they should do unto you."

To drop all irony, surely this was one of those stages of civilization at which one might well say that, if it was to stop there, it was a pity that it had ever got so far. I have had to study books and methods of work of the eighteenth century a good deal, French chiefly; and I must say that the impression made on me by that study is that the eighteenth century artisan must have been a terrible product of civilization, and quite in a condition to give rise to *hopes*—of the torch, the pike, and the guillotine.

However, civilization was not going to stop there; having turned the man into a machine, the next stage for commerce to aim at was to contrive machines which would widely dispense with human labour; nor was this aim altogether disappointed.

Now, at first sight it would seem that having got the workman into such a plight as he was, as the slave of division of labour, this new invention of machines which should free him from a part of his labour at least, could be nothing to him but an unmixed blessing. Doubtless it will prove to have been so in the end, when certain institutions have been swept away which most people now look on as eternal; but a longish time has passed during which the workman's hopes of civilization have been disappointed, for those who invented the machines, or rather who profited by their invention, did not aim at the saving of labour in the sense of reducing the labour which each man had to do, but, first taking it for granted that every workman would have to work as long as he could stand up to it, aimed, under those conditions of labour, at producing the utmost amount of goods which they could sell at a profit.

Need I dwell on the fact that, under these circumstances, the invention of the machines has benefited the workman but little even to this day?

Nay, at first they made his position worse than it had been: for, being thrust on the world very suddenly, they distinctly brought about an industrial revolution, changing everything suddenly and completely; industrial productiveness was increased prodigiously, but so far from the workers reaping the benefit of this, they were thrown out of work in enormous numbers, while those who were still employed were reduced from the position of skilled artisans to that of unskilled labourers: the aims of their masters being, as I said, to make a profit, they did not trouble themselves about this as a class, but took it for granted that it was something that couldn't be helped and didn't hurt *them*: nor did they think of offering to the workers that

compensation for harassed interests which they have since made
a point of claiming so loudly for themselves.

This was the state of things which followed on the conclusion
of European peace, and even that peace itself rather made matters
worse than better, by the sudden cessation of all war industries,
and the throwing on to the market [of] many thousands of
soldiers and sailors: in short, at no period of English history was
the condition of the workers worse than in the early years of the
nineteenth century.

There seem during this period to have been two currents of
hope that had reference to the working classes: the first affected
the masters, the second the men.

In England, and, in what I am saying of this period, I am
chiefly thinking of England, the hopes of the richer classes ran
high; and no wonder; for England had by this time become the
mistress of the markets of the world, and also, as the people of
that period were never weary of boasting, the workshop of the
world: the increase in the riches of the country was enormous,
even at the early period I am thinking of now—prior to '48, I
mean—though it increased much more speedily in times that we
have all seen: but part of the jubilant hopes of this newly rich
man concerned his servants, the instruments of his fortune: it
was hoped that the population in general would grow wiser,
better educated, thriftier, more industrious, more comfortable;
for which hope there was surely some foundation, since man's
mastery over the forces of Nature was growing yearly towards
completion; but you see these benevolent gentlemen supposed
that these hopes would be realized perhaps by some unexplained
magic as aforesaid, or perhaps by the working-classes, *at their own
expense*, by the exercise of virtues supposed to be specially suited
to their condition, and called, by their masters, "thrift" and
"industry." For this latter supposition there was no foundation:
indeed, the poor wretches who were thrown out of work by
the triumphant march of commerce had perforce worn thrift

threadbare, and could hardly better their exploits in *that* direction; while as to those who worked in the factories, or who formed the fringe of labour elsewhere, industry was no new gospel to them, since they already worked as long as they could work without dying at the loom, the spindle, or the stithy. They for their part had their hopes, vague enough as to their ultimate aim, but expressed in the passing day by a very obvious tendency to revolt: this tendency took various forms, which I cannot dwell on here, but settled down at last into Chartism: about which I must speak a few words. But first I must mention, I can scarce do more, the honoured name of Robert Owen, as representative of the nobler hopes of his day, just as More was of his, and the lifter of the torch of Socialism amidst the dark days of the confusion consequent on the reckless greed of the early period of the great factory industries.

That the conditions under which men lived could affect his life and his deeds infinitely, that not selfish greed and ceaseless contention, but brotherhood and co-operation were the bases of true society, was the gospel which he preached and also practised with a single-heartedness, devotion, and fervour of hope which have never been surpassed: he was the embodied hope of the days when the advance of knowledge and the sufferings of the people thrust revolutionary hope upon those thinkers who were not in some form or other in the pay of the sordid masters of society.

As to the Chartist agitation, there is this to be said of it, that it was thoroughly a working-class movement, and it was caused by the simplest and most powerful of all causes—hunger. It is noteworthy that it was strongest, especially in its earlier days, in the Northern and Midland manufacturing districts—that is, in the places which felt the distress caused by the industrial revolution most sorely and directly; it sprang up with particular vigour in the years immediately following the great Reform Bill; and it has been remarked that disappointment of the hopes

which that measure had cherished had something to do with
its bitterness. As it went on, obvious causes for failure were
developed in it; self-seeking leadership; futile discussion of the
means of making the change, before organization of the party
was perfected; blind fear of ultimate consequences on the part of
some, blind disregard to immediate consequences on the part of
others; these were the surface reasons for its failure: but it would
have triumphed over all these and accomplished revolution in
England, if it had not been for causes deeper and more vital than
these. Chartism differed from mere Radicalism in being a class
movement; but its aim was after all political rather than social.
The Socialism of Robert Owen fell short of its object because it
did not understand that, as long as there is a privileged class in
possession of the executive power, they will take good care that
their economical position, which enables them to live on the
unpaid labour of the people, is not tampered with: the hopes of
the Chartists were disappointed because they did not understand
that true political freedom is impossible to people who are
economically enslaved: there is no first and second in these
matters, the two must go hand in hand together: we cannot live
as we will, and as we should, as long as we allow people to *govern*
us whose interest it is that we should live as *they* will, and by no
means as we should; neither is it any use claiming the right to
manage our own business unless we are prepared to have some
business of our own: these two aims united mean the furthering
of the class struggle till all classes are abolished—the divorce of
one from the other is fatal to any hope of social advancement.

Chartism therefore, though a genuine popular movement,
was incomplete in its aims and knowledge; the time was not yet
come and it could not triumph openly; but it would be a mistake
to say that it failed utterly: at least it kept alive the holy flame of
discontent; it made it possible for us to attain to the political goal
of democracy, and thereby to advance the cause of the people by

the gain of a stage from whence could be seen the fresh gain to be aimed at.

I have said that the time for revolution had not then come: the great wave of commercial success went on swelling, and though the capitalists would if they had dared have engrossed the whole of the advantages thereby gained at the expense of their wage slaves, the Chartist revolt warned them that it was not safe to attempt it. They were *forced* to try to allay discontent by palliative measures. They had to allow Factory Acts to be passed regulating the hours and conditions of labour of women and children, and consequently of men also in some of the more important and consolidated industries; they were *forced* to repeal the ferocious laws against combination among the workmen; so that the Trades Unions won for themselves a legal position and became a power in the labour question, and were able by means of strikes and threats of strikes to regulate the wages granted to the workers, and to raise the standard of livelihood for a certain part of the skilled workmen and the labourers associated with them: though the main part of the unskilled, including agricultural workmen, were no better off than before.

Thus was damped down the flame of a discontent vague in its aims, and passionately crying out for what, if granted, it could not have used: twenty years ago any one hinting at the possibility of serious class discontent in this country would have been looked upon as a madman; in fact, the well-to-do and cultivated were quite unconscious (as many still are) that there was any class distinction in this country other than what was made by the rags and cast clothes of feudalism, which in a perfunctory manner they still attacked.

There was no sign of revolutionary feeling in England twenty years ago: the middle class were so rich that they had no need to hope for anything—but a heaven which they did not believe in: the well-to-do working men did not hope, since they were not pinched and had no means of learning their degraded position:

and lastly, the drudges of the proletariat had such hope as charity, the hospital, the workhouse, and kind death at last could offer them.

In this stock-jobbers' heaven let us leave our dear countrymen for a little, while I say a few words about the affairs of the people on the continent of Europe. Things were not quite so smooth for the fleecer there: Socialist thinkers and writers had arisen about the same time as Robert Owen; St. Simon, Proudhon, Fourier and his followers kept up the traditions of hope in the midst of a *bourgeois* world. Amongst these Fourier is the one that calls for most attention: since his doctrine of the necessity and possibility of making labour attractive is one which Socialism can by no means do without. France also kept up the revolutionary and insurrectionary tradition, the result of something like hope still fermenting amongst the proletariat: she fell at last into the clutches of a second Cæsarism developed by the basest set of sharpers, swindlers, and harlots that ever insulted a country, and of whom our own happy *bourgeois* at home made heroes and heroines: the hideous open corruption of Parisian society, to which, I repeat, our respectable classes accorded heartfelt sympathy, was finally swept away by the horrors of a race war: the defeats and disgraces of this war developed, on the one hand, an increase in the wooden implacability and baseness of the French *bourgeois*, but on the other made way for revolutionary hope to spring again, from which resulted the attempt to establish society on the basis of the freedom of labour, which we call the Commune of Paris of 1871. Whatever mistakes or imprudences were made in this attempt, and all wars blossom thick with such mistakes, I will leave the reactionary enemies of the people's cause to put forward: the immediate and obvious result was the slaughter of thousands of brave and honest revolutionists at the hands of the respectable classes, the loss in fact of an army for the popular cause. But we may be sure that the results of the Commune will not stop there: to all

Socialists that heroic attempt will give hope and ardour in the
cause as long as it is to be won; we feel as though the Paris
workman had striven to bring the day-dawn for us, and had lifted
up the sun's rim over the horizon, never to set in utter darkness
again: of such attempts one must say, that though those who
perished in them might have been put in a better place in the
battle, yet after all brave men never die for nothing, when they
die for principle.

Let us shift from France to Germany before we get back to
England again, and conclude with a few words about our hopes
at the present day. To Germany we owe the school of economists,
at whose head stands the name of Karl Marx, who have made
modern Socialism what it is: the earlier Socialist writers and
preachers based their hopes on man being taught to see the desir-
ableness of co-operation taking the place of competition, and
adopting the change voluntarily and consciously, and they trusted
to schemes more or less artificial being tried and accepted,
although such schemes were necessarily constructed out of the
materials which capitalistic society offered: but the new school,
starting with an historical view of what had been, and seeing that
a law of evolution swayed all events in it, was able to point out to
us that the evolution was still going on, and that, whether
Socialism be desirable or not, it is at least inevitable. Here then
was at last a hope of a different kind to any that had gone before
it; and the German and Austrian workmen were not slow to
learn the lesson founded on this theory; from being one of the
most backward countries in Europe in the movement, before
Lassalle started his German workman's party in 1863, Germany
soon became the leader in it: Bismarck's repressive law has only
acted on opinion there, as the roller does to the growing grass—
made it firmer and stronger; and whatever vicissitudes may be
the fate of the party as a party, there can be no doubt that
Socialistic opinion is firmly established there, and that when the
time is ripe for it that opinion will express itself in action.

Now, in all I have been saying, I have been wanting you to trace the fact that, ever since the establishment of commercialism on the ruins of feudality, there has been growing a steady feeling on the part of the workers that they are a class dealt with as a class, and in like manner to deal with others; and that as this class feeling has grown, so also has grown with it a consciousness of the antagonism between their class and the class which employs it, as the phrase goes; that is to say, which lives by means of its labour.

Now it is just this growing consciousness of the fact that as long as there exists in society a propertied class living on the labour of a propertyless one, there *must* be a struggle always going on between those two classes—it is just the dawning knowledge of this fact which should show us what civilization can hope for—namely, transformation into true society, in which there will no longer be classes with their necessary struggle for existence and superiority: for the antagonism of classes which began in all simplicity between the master and the chattel slave of ancient society, and was continued between the feudal lord and the serf of mediæval society, has gradually become the contention between the capitalist developed from the workmen of the last-named period, and the wage-earner: in the former struggle the rise of the artisan and villeinage tenant created a new class, the middle class, while the place of the old serf was filled by the propertyless labourer, with whom the middle class, which has absorbed the aristocracy, is now face to face: the struggle between the classes therefore is once again a simple one, as in the days of the classical peoples; but since there is no longer any strong race left out of civilization, as in the time of the disruption of Rome, the whole struggle in all its simplicity between those who have and those who lack is *within* civilization.

Moreover, the capitalist or modern slave-owner has been forced by his very success, as we have seen, to organize his slaves, the wage-earners, into a co-operation for production so arranged that it requires little but his own elimination to make it a foundation for communal life: in the teeth also of the experience of past ages, he has been compelled to allow a modicum of education to the propertyless, and has not even been able to deprive them wholly of political rights; his own advance in wealth and power has bred for him the very enemy who is doomed to make an end of him.

But will there be any new class to take the place of the present proletariat when that has triumphed, as it must do, over the present privileged class? We cannot foresee the future, but we may fairly hope not: at least we cannot see any signs of such a new class forming. It is impossible to see how destruction of privilege can stop short of absolute equality of condition; pure Communism is the logical education from the imperfect form of the new society, which is generally differentiated from it as Socialism.

Meantime, it is this simplicity and directness of the growing contest which above all things presents itself as a terror to the conservative instinct of the present day. Many among the middle class who are sincerely grieved and shocked at the condition of the proletariat which civilization has created, and even alarmed by the frightful inequalities which it fosters, do nevertheless shudder back from the idea of the class struggle, and strive to shut their eyes to the fact that it is going on. They try to think that peace is not only possible, but natural, between the two classes, the very essence of whose existence is that each can only thrive by what it manages to force the other to yield to it. They propose to themselves the impossible problem of raising the inferior or exploited classes into a position in which they will cease to struggle against the superior classes, while the latter will not cease to exploit them. This absurd position drives them into the concoction of schemes for bettering the condition of the working classes at their own expense, some of them futile, some merely fantastic; or they may be divided again into those which point out the advantages and pleasures of involuntary asceticism, and reactionary plans for importing the conditions of the production and life of the Middle Ages (wholly misunderstood by them, by the way) into the present system of the capitalist farmer, the great industries, and the universal world-market. Some see a solution of the social problem in sham co-operation, which is merely an improved form of joint-stockery: others preach thrift to (precarious) incomes of eighteen shillings a week, and industry to men killing themselves by inches in working overtime, or to men whom the labour-market has rejected as not wanted: others beg the proletarians not to breed so fast; an injunction the compliance with which might be at first of advantage to the proletarians themselves in their present condition, but would certainly undo the capitalists, if it were carried to any lengths, and would lead through ruin and misery to the violent outbreak of the very revolution which these timid people are so anxious to forego.

Then there are others who, looking back on the past, and perceiving that the workmen of the Middle Ages lived in more comfort and self-respect than ours do, even though they were subjected to the class rule of men who were looked on as another order of beings than they, think that if those conditions of life could be reproduced under our better political conditions the question would be solved for a time at least. Their schemes may be summed up in attempts, more or less preposterously futile, to graft a class of independent peasants on our system of wages and capital. They do not understand that this system of independent workmen, producing almost entirely for the consumption of themselves and their neighbours, and exploited by the upper classes by obvious taxes on their labour, which was not otherwise organized or interfered with by the exploiters, was what in past times took the place of our system, in which the workers sell their labour in the competitive market to masters who have in

their hands the whole organization of the markets, and that these
two systems are mutually destructive.

Others again believe in the possibility of starting from our
present workhouse system, for the raising of the lowest part of
the working population into a better condition, but do not
trouble themselves as to the position of the workers who are
fairly above the condition of pauperism, or consider what part
they will play in the contest for a better livelihood. And, lastly,
quite a large number of well-intentioned persons belonging to
the richer classes believe, that in a society that compels competition for livelihood, and holds out to the workers as a stimulus
to exertion the hope of their rising into a monopolist class of
non-producers, it is yet possible to "moralize" capital (to use a
slang phrase of the Positivists): that is to say, that a sentiment
imported from a religion which looks upon another world as the
true sphere of action for mankind, will override the necessities of
our daily life in this world. This curious hope is founded on the
feeling that a sentiment antagonistic to the full development of
commercialism exists and is gaining ground, and that this
sentiment is an independent growth of the ethics of the present
epoch. As a matter of fact, admitting its existence, as I think we
must do, it is the birth of the sense of insecurity which is the
shadow cast before by the approaching dissolution of modern
society founded on wage-slavery.

The greater part of these schemes aim, though seldom with
the consciousness of their promoters, at the creation of a new
middle-class out of the wage-earning class, and at their expense,
just as the present middle-class was developed out of the serf-
population of the early Middle Ages. It may be possible that such
a *further* development of the middle-class lies before us, but it will
not be brought about by any such artificial means as the above-
mentioned schemes. If it comes at all, it must be produced by
events, which at present we cannot foresee, acting on our

commercial system, and revivifying for a little time, maybe, the Capitalist Society which now seems sickening towards its end.

For what is visible before us in these days is the competitive commercial system killing itself by its own force: profits lessening, businesses growing bigger and bigger, the small employer of labour thrust out of his function, and the aggregation of capital increasing the numbers of the lower middle-class from above rather than from below, by driving the smaller manufacturer into the position of a mere servant to the bigger. The productivity of labour also increasing out of all proportion to the capacity of the capitalists to manage the market or deal with the labour supply: lack of employment therefore becoming chronic, and discontent therewithal.

All this on the one hand. On the other, the workman claiming everywhere political equality, which cannot long be denied; and education spreading, so that what between the improvement in the education of the working-class and the continued amazing fatuity of that of the upper classes, there is a distinct tendency to equalization here; and, as I have hinted above, all history shows us what a danger to society may be a class at once educated and socially degraded: though, indeed, no history has yet shown us—what is swiftly advancing upon us—a class which, though it shall have attained knowledge, shall lack utterly the refinement and self-respect which come from the union of knowledge with leisure and ease of life. The growth of such a class may well make the "cultured" people of to-day tremble.

Whatever, therefore, of unforeseen and unconceived-of may lie in the womb of the future, there is nothing visible before us but a decaying system, with no outlook but ever-increasing entanglement and blindness, and a new system, Socialism, the hope of which is ever growing clearer in men's minds—a system which not only sees how labour can be freed from its present fetters, and organized unwastefully, so as to produce the greatest possible amount of wealth for the community and for every member of it, but which bears with it its own ethics and religion and æsthetics: that is the hope and promise of a new and higher life in all ways. So that even if those unforeseen economical events above spoken of were to happen, and put off for a while the end of our Capitalist system, the latter would drag itself along as an anomaly cursed by all, a mere clog on the aspirations of humanity.

It is not likely that it will come to that: in all probability the logical outcome of the latter days of Capitalism will go step by step with its actual history: while all men, even its declared enemies, will be working to bring Socialism about, the aims of those who have learned to believe in the certainty and beneficence of its advent will become clearer, their methods for realizing it clearer also, and at last ready to hand. Then will come that open acknowledgement for the necessity of the change (an acknowledgement coming from the intelligence of civilization) which is commonly called Revolution. It is no use prophesying as to the events which will accompany that revolution, but to a reasonable man it seems unlikely to the last degree, or we will say impossible, that a moral sentiment will induce the proprietary classes—those who live by *owning* the means of production which the unprivileged classes must needs *use*—to yield up this privilege uncompelled; all one can hope is that they will see the implicit threat of compulsion in the events of the day, and so yield with a good grace to the terrible necessity of forming part of a world in which all, including themselves, will work honestly and live easily.

* I suppose he was speaking of the frame houses of Kent.

EARLY ENGLAND

1886

I am no patriot as the word is generally used; and yet I am not ashamed to say that as for the face of the land we live in I love it with something of the passion of a lover: that is to say more than its beauty or interest in relation to other parts of the earth warrants. Perhaps that is because I am in the habit of looking at things that pass before my eyes; (which I think has now ceased to be a common habit) and connecting their present outward seeming with times gone by and times to come.

Again I will not say that the past history of our country is of interest so absorbing as to make us forget that of other countries: nay I know that there is a certain want of romance about it, compared with other stories of national life, and that as it goes on it tends ever more and more to the commonplace. But to us who are come of the actors of it and live amongst the scenes where it was enacted it has a special interest which consecrates it. Egotism you will say: well so it is, but under our present conditions and perhaps for centuries to come an egotism which is natural, and if we only keep it in order by cultivating our sense of justice to other nations, and our insight and interest in the history of the whole world this affection for [our] own parish and the people of it may even [come] to [be] useful to us and others.

I make these excuses because, as you see by the title of my lecture I am going today to confine my story within the limits of our own island stowed away in an odd corner of the world. What

I want to do is to give you a picture of what has been in England dwelling almost entirely on the most characteristic periods of its history, as those which lend themselves most to such a picture; to say a few words on its present condition so familiar to us all, so misunderstood by most, so sad to some; and to finish by hazarding some guesses at what it will be like in times to come: painting a picture in the air, this last will be I know: and I ask you to receive it as such.

Now I intend to say scarcely anything about the men of the earlier times before Caesar crossed the Thames up at Walton yonder, and his dark, short, close-knit soldiers plunged into the perilous woods of Middlesex on the other side. Of those earlier days you may however remember that the records of them are chiefly to be found on the great chalk downs that run along and athwart southern England; this will help you to picture to yourselves, the lowlands covered with marsh and tangled forest, good only for hunting such beasts as could live there, badger, red deer, wild swine, wolf, squirrel, and the like; the untended rivers often spreading out in mere swamp and morass, and the parts habitable by man the year round the downs, or the slopes of the hills on which sheep could pasture: there dwelt the earlier, not earliest, inhabitants of Britain, tribe fighting with tribe doubtless, and therefore raising earthworks on the brows of the hills in which the whole tribe could gather and drive their flocks and herds for safety: several races doubtless have used these rude but effective fortresses; as for instance the great earthwork, called Uffington Castle, which from the wall of the Wiltshire downs looks over the fair rich valley of the Thames: there along the ridge of the hill behind it runs a Roman road, while a furlong from it on the hill-ridge is the tomb of some chief of the earlier people, which to our Saxon forefathers, when they first came there, seemed so remote and mysterious that they named it by one of the earliest of their Gods, the Vulcan of the North, and called it the cave of Wayland the Smith.

There also they raised holy places, concerning which endless guesses have been made, which probably must forever remain guesses; but at least one may say this of them that the earliest historical people that found them there seem little nearer to their builders than we do. Most impressive they are and also most instructive even amidst their history; the man must be hard to move indeed who is not moved who as he turns the corner of one of our commonplace English highways comes suddenly across that marvellous hedge of grey stones that our Saxon ancestors called Stonehenge: or looks from the great circular Earthwork of Avebury on the little old village that lies within it, where the cottages are cheek by jowl with the few remaining stones of the ancient temple there: lying close by the huge barrow of Silbury, the hills about all dotted with graves of the early chieftains; the mysterious Wansdjke drawn across the downs at the back; wherein even now the horses are tethered when the yearly traditional horse fair takes place at 'Tan Hill.' And lastly once more the Roman road running through it all towards Bath, just swerved a little by the huge mass of Silbury: a familiar place to my boyhood; yet a holy place indeed. There is a pretty story current of Aubrey, the Wiltshire archaeologist of the 17th century, that one day as he was out on the downs hunting or coursing, he suddenly came across the Earthwork of Avebury and the Stones of the Temple, then much more numerous than they are now. He drew rein and sat there musing and at last turned and rode home soberly, and from that day foreswore hawk and hound and became a diligent and useful archaeologist.

Well, perhaps the life of these earlier peoples dwelling on the high lands amidst their flocks and herds in a very elementary society tending toward the tribal condition, and struggling slowly into a more elaborate life and greater command over the powers of nature, is easier to picture than the following periods, when there were many peoples in Britain and many different conditions of progress, the time when the Roman servitude first began:

many huge tracts of unsettled land [were] yet left; many of the
tribes were still in a savage state; but there were kingdoms,
probably Gaulish, on the East and Southeast which were not only
clear of the savage state but could scarcely perhaps be called
barbarian even; and tillage though interrupted by the wastes and
forests was widely spread; the population generally was ages past
the men of Avebury and Stonehenge. Into this population the
Romans brought 'the blessings of civilization,' and destroyed the
chances of the natural development of the British tribes, slowly
hammering to pieces all resistance, till they had established the
great tax-gathering machine the Roman bureaucracy, the great
curse of the ancient world, as our commercial market-hunting
bureaucracy is the great curse of the modern world.

On the miserable period of this Roman servitude I will not
dwell: the one gift that the Imperial tax-gatherers gave to the
island was roads made through it for the safe-conduct of their
bum-bailiffs, which to this day are useful both to thieves,
lawyers, and honest men: for the rest it was a matter of course
that they should deprive the unlucky people of all character and
public spirit and so make them an easy prey to the first comers
who were necessitous and bold enough to take hold of the land
which it was no one's business to defend.

The necessitous and bold newcomers were ready by this time:
from the shores of the Baltic and the North Sea came the tribes
of the English, the Jutes, and the Saxons coolly risking everything
in their half-decked or undecked luggers, the men who had long
been a terror to the Roman provincials, who had learned to
expect them on the coast when the weather was so bad that no
civilized keel could keep the sea.

These were the men that now fell upon our islands and made
a new set of pictures for us to look on. And before I go further I
should like to clear your minds of a misconception which some
persons by a happy exercise of ignorance and cant have led us
into. These men of the earlier world were rough, predatory,

cruel, or at least of ungovernable passions which led them into cruelty; but there is no parallel between them and the offscourings of our commercial civilization as certain fifth-rate romanticists are apt to try to make us believe: the ruffians who are the quite worthy pioneers of American or English colonial civilization are to the backbone commercial; they are stock-jobbers down on their luck, and only want a month or two of the ordinary varnish of civilization to become respectable members of Society; i.e. thieves under the protection and encouragement of the laws: and take note that their distinguishing characteristic is 'vulgarity' a quality which in the full signification of the very modern word is a creation of this century.

Now if you ask me how I know that these terrible sea rovers who founded the English nation amidst rapine and bloodshed in these islands were free from this foulest of qualities I can tell you, first that they bore with them a literature, unwritten of course, but fragments of which having been afterwards written down are still left us: and doubtless these early poems at least, in which language is uncorrupted and has not yet learned to speak with the double tongue, reflect the mind of the people which produced them; the epic of Beowulf is worthy of a great people for its sincerity of language and beauty of expression, and nowhere lacks the epic quality of putting clear pictures before the readers' eyes; nor is there anything in it coarse, ignoble, or degrading; on the contrary it breathes the very spirit of courageous freedom: to live is good and to die is good if you are valiant and faithful and if you reckon great deeds and the fair fame that comes of them of more account than a few more short years of a trembler's life upon the earth. This is the simple ethic of our forefathers, and in these poems is so set forth that it is clear they really believed it and that in consequence life amidst all its sufferings and hardships was a continuous poem to them. In later times it has become a commonplace and is no longer believed, therefore except for moments of spasmodic excitement life is dull [and]

shapeless, so that some in their foolish despair will ask, is it
worth the living? Clearly it is not unless we can live fearlessly
and confident of our immortality not as individuals but as a part
of the great corporation of humanity; and that I say was the faith
of our forefathers.

And this faith of which these glorious poems are the simple
expression was itself bred of the conditions of life to which the
race had attained: the hideous card-sharping border ruffians of
America and the colonies are terrible to friend and foe alike, pure
individualists, they have nothing to do with anything except the
immediate satisfaction of their own impulses; but the Teutonic
tribes that followed the footsteps of the Roman tax-gatherers
were corporate bodies of men united into artificial families for
self-preservation and the satisfaction of the mutual needs of their
members; and these families again were at the point of federating
if they had not already federated into a bigger body 'the people'
(*theod*). 'No rights without duties, no duties without rights' was
in fact the principle which their constitution strove to *illustrate
within the limits of the corporation of the family the gens and the theod*: so
that within those limits it was to their foes rather than their
friends that they were terrible. That limitation is necessary
because outside their tribe or people it was war, and war brought
prisoners sometimes and those prisoners became property and
were called thralls. That is the blot on the constitution of our
forefathers as it was of the ancient Greeks.

Now you must understand that the civilization of which the
Roman Empire was a corruption was founded on the institution
of the city: which means not the mere stones and mortar of the
dwellings of the citizens, but the corporation of which they each
formed a part, yet again the corporation fixed in a certain holy
place: the city was the unit of civilization; outside it was nothing
but confusion. The external aspect of this city-worship, for it was
no less, the Roman domination had retained everywhere, even in
such outlying spots as Britain. But the tribes who gradually

supplanted the Roman Empire on the contrary had no idea of a city, this of the fixed abode for the gens or tribe or *theod*, the field amidst the forest rather is the idea of the dwelling of the germanic tribe. This of course meant a lower form of the development of Society; but into the Society of the City these tribes never developed, but their tribalism melted into the society of feudalism and the Church instead. And it was only where the influence of the Roman Empire was strong that any semblance of the ancient city life lasted into the Middle Ages: in England for instance only those towns have any traces of it that were founded by the Romans: and it is interesting to note that it you come into any town which has many parishes such a town is almost certainly Roman in origin: e.g. Norwich [and] Yarmouth.

The Anglo-Saxons [who] then came to this country in the condition of barbarism [were] the most advanced toward that ancient civilization, which faded away altogether before they could develop into it. Their want of sympathy with the city life in the first years of their occupation was almost as marked as that of the gypsy or the Bedouin for house life. When they took one of the towns of the Romanized Britons they could not use it; they sacked it and burned it, and went back again to their own simpler habitations: you must think of them then at first as dwelling in farm-steads along the rivers or the sea shore, or in clearings of the woods, in that field amid the forest of which I was speaking: thus sprung up those villages with English names all over the country, each one of which was the settlement of some family or other; and curiously enough sometimes their names used for constitutional divisions have outlasted the place itself (hundred of Ossulton—where is it?) nevertheless there was, if there is not now some stead which was founded by one Oswald and was therefore called his town. That very word [town] which we now use as the generic term for a collection of houses and a biggish one at that shows by change from its original meaning how far removed the first English were from city life: in Scotland the word is or lately was used to designate a farmstead merely or the house in it; while further north the word is still used in its original sense of the cultivated field around a dwelling as contrasted with the out-meadows or mere uncultured pasture lands.

Thus then did the tribes from the Baltic found the English nation in our island, and lived at first not so very differently from their fathers as they made their way through the great forests of mid-Europe: their history as read in the books is but a series of battles with the resisting Britons or chief with chief of their own blood; yet doubt it not that all the time their home life went on with something of dignity under the constitution of which I have hinted: in which every free man had to take his share of responsibility for carrying on the business of the Community. But as time passed and the limits of the rule of the different Chieftains got more defined, the tribal feeling waned: the Chiefs and Kings, also, as Mr. Elton says began to inhabit the towns that the Romans had founded, and the aspect of the great building works of that most solid-building of peoples struck a chord of melancholy in the hearts of their poets: here are a few lines from a poem called The Ruin preserved in a volume written in Athelstane's time, the sentiment of which differs little from that of our own time:–

> Wondrous the wall-stone that Weird hath broken ... the roof-tree riven, the grey gates despoiled. Often that wall withstood Raeghar and Readfah, chieftain after chieftain rising in storm. Bright was the burgh-place many the princely halls, and high was the roof of gold... And the court is dreary, and the crowned roof lies low in the shadow of the purple arch. Princes of old time joyous and gold-bright and splendidly-decked, proud and with wine elate, in war gear shone. They looked on their treasures, on silver and gems and on stones of price, and on this bright burgh of their broad realm. The stone court stands, the hot stream hath whelmed it, there where the bath was hot on the breast.

To get done with this matter of the towns I may say also that other towns besides these Roman cities got founded, some as the surroundings of Burgs or strong places, some as merchant towns.

But now the Feudal system which was destined to embrace the customary law of the Germanic tribes and the remains of Roman authority, mingled here perhaps with some Easternism from New Rome, began to creep over the country: I tried to put before you some time ago the way in which feudality naturally developed from the customs of the tribes [that] conquered the kindred peoples of Scandinavia, and much the same thing went on in England, so that by Athelstane's time there certainly was established a kind of feudality here; and from that time onward England was destined to be no longer isolated from the more Romanized nations of the Continent. Moreover from the time when Christianity first came amongst them some shades of Rome does as it were seem to hang over the Early English which the Scandinavian kingdoms were free from. As far as our early literature is concerned that was a great misfortune. The history and mythology of Scandinavia was enshrined in the rough casket of Iceland, and though at the time when it was written the people of that island had been converted to Christianity, yet except where the subject-matter positively demands it there is no sign of the new religion having made any practical impression on the writers, and though monks and priests took their part in this literature, works written in Latin are rare. But in England it was different; the literature was mostly in the hands of the monks, there are not many works left us in the vernacular, and of those several of the most important are paraphrases of bible stories or at least pieces founded on the Christian mythology of which we have so much in other forms. There are in Anglo-Saxon in short none of those pieces of local history told in a terse and amazingly realistic and dramatic style which bring back to us Iceland and Norway in the eleventh century: and what is still more unlucky we have lost the account of the mythology of the North from the Low German branch of the great Teutonic race: it is the feeblest and slenderest branch of the Goths that have been the story tellers of the race and not the Germans or the English: Odin we know in his goings out and comings in, but Wotan and Woden are but names to us. And it is a pity indeed; for what there is left of the poems of the ancient English (apart from Beowulf) show[s] tokens of the highest and most elevating capacities: no lyrics in the English language are more beautiful, and few indeed as full of feeling and true poetic passion as some of those preserved in that "Exeter book" I have already mentioned.

The turning of the rude kings and chieftains of an outlying island toward what was once the centre of the civilized world, and was still the centre of Christianity, has to the mere romanticist something striking and even pathetic about it: the stream of pilgrims daring the dangers that then beset the traveller through central Europe to reach the Eternal City; the kings and queens that laid their crowns at the feet of the holy father, and died in the odour of sanctity there: an English Bishop (St. Boniface) the apostle of the heathen Wends of Prussia and their martyr. And yet all that pomp of religion does not make up to me for the loss of the stories I might have had of how the folk of Middlesex ate and drank and loved and quarrelled and met their death in the 10th century.

But once more the time was coming when England was to be a part of Europe; and meantime it seems in spite of the stout men that dwelt here, she could not hold her own before the *Furor Normanorum* that stirred up all Europe that lay anywhere near the sea. By the time the tribes were fairly settled and the development of the *theod* into a nation under a feudal king was going on, the Northmen had fallen on the island, and from that time till the Norman conquest gave it no rest except when the whole country was in their power: the English called them generically Danes but the first comers were from Norway a branch of the great stream that overran Europe: conquering Normandy, making yearly inroads right up into France, and North Germany:

the men who carved Norse kingdoms out of Ireland, settled Iceland, and upheld the throne of the Emperor of the East. Against this energy, bred doubtless of necessity, the English could make but little head: the wide extent of sea-board with its numerous harbours beat them; and you must remember that they had to meet people who were born seamen while the English of that day and for centuries afterwards were not a seafaring people. So that for a time it seemed likely that the whole of society would be broken up by these bold strong-thieves. For the invasions of this early period were not for conquest but for pillage; 'lying out' was as regular a business with the northern landholders and yeomen as their ordinary field-work: it is told of an Earl of the Orkneys that he had two regular viking cruises in the year; the first after the seed was sown which he called his spring cruise, the second after it was harvested, called his autumn cruise: some of the vikings went into partnership with the kings and shared the proceeds both of peaceful chaffer and fighting: with the most spirited, well-bred young men it was thought proper that they should go through a viking cruise for one or two summers, such as our young gentlemen and noblemen used some 100 years ago to think it necessary to do the grand tour. Once again you must not fall into the mistake of picturing the men who partly lived on this woeful industry as being either like the brigands of romance or the sordid pirates of more modern times even Captain[s] Teach and Kidd, or like the chivalry of the later Middle Ages: the greater part of the men who harried England were when they got back home respectable agriculturalists; yeomen, or at least landlords who were not ashamed to work with their own hands: Gunnar, one warrior, is represented as sowing his cornfield; Arnkel a very great man in Iceland, mending his own gate: King Sigurd the father of King Harald the Terrible who fell near York before our King Harald, is found in his hayfield helping his men get in his hay harvest: the warriors were shipwrights, house-builders and armourers, and almost every one could [s]ettle a

copy of verses on occasion. They lived under an elaborate system
of laws which later on were written out at length, and doubtless
had it not been for their narrow and barren lands their fierce
valour would have smouldered away amidst the peaceful occupations of the land: the sea that fed them drew them on to way-
laying its watery roads.

Well whatever they were at home they were a fearful visitation
in the countries that they used as their hunting grounds: the first
thing they did after landing on the coast was to throw themselves
on any body of men that showed fight in order to get horses; for
oddly enough they were as much horsemen as seamen: or they
would row up the rivers, very much higher than we should
expect them to have gone, and throw up an earthwork: you will
read such entries in the Saxon Chronicle as 'This year the Host
sailed up the Seine to Paris and sat a year there.' Another year
they went up the Marne far beyond Paris. They rowed high up
the Lea and entrenched themselves there against Alfred another
time. Sometimes a band would ally itself with the Welsh chieftains, sometimes with the Scots. In short the host of the Heathen
was a ceaseless plague in the land and [as] I said seemed about to
reduce it to a state of mere confusion when there appeared on
the scene a man whose pure fame no amount of legend can
obscure, and the interest in whom must always win one's heart
however much his name has been hackneyed, the man born at
Wantage in Berkshire, Alfred the son of Aethelwulf; of whom
one must say that there was one other man of genius who has sat
on the throne in England and that is Oliver Cromwell, and he
betrayed the cause which he had in charge and mourned by his
friends rather before he died than when he died. But Alfred's
fame was pure and stainless and both in his shortcomings and his
successes he was human and sympathetic. Yes I think we must
call him the one sole man of genius who ever held an official
position among the English.

Well he began his contest with the Vikings with some hope of success, fought nine great battles in one year says the S[axon] Ch[ronicler]: one of them in which he and his brother Aethelred defeated the heathen and slew Baejsecg and Halfdan their kings, and was fought at Ashdown some mile from that Uffington Castle I have told you of, and as his men came back from the fight, they amused themselves by cutting away the turf from the slope of the chalk hill so that the white showed on the green in the figure of a white horse, the beast of their banner done so as to satisfy their imaginations of the thing: and from that day to this it has abided there unchanged: and one day this summer I sat on him and looked down on that fair plain of the Thames, changed enough in outward seeming from the days of Alfred but how much more in the ways of life of the people who dwell there!

The battle of Ashdown was pretty much the end of the first act of Alfred's struggle; the second was a time of defeat and disaster; but he struggled out of it, and again made head against the host, defeated it over and over again, made some sort of terms with the leaders, followed up all who resisted untiringly, and at last triumphed; the date of Ashdown is 871: in 886 the Chronicler writes "In this same year Alfred restored London; and all the Anglo-race turned to him that were not in the bondage of the Danish men." Much fighting there was afterwards, but in 897 the Chronicler could write as if the war was over: "Thanks be to God the Host had not utterly broken up the Anglo Race." So that England remained England, though the Danish kingdoms of Northumbria and East Anglia were still a thorn in its side. Successful kings followed Alfred, who however had plenty of fighting with the Danes, till at last Edgar was acknowledged over-king of England, and received homage of the Welsh, Scotch, and Danish kings in England. It seems pretty clear that by his time that un-Romanized feudal system I have spoken of was fully established in the country. The king was no longer the head of a clan or even of a people or *theod*; but the master of the land giving fiefs to his earls and thanes, who in their turn gave them to their free men. Edgar (died 975) as he was the first over-king of England, was also the last successful one: the Northmen were again at war with the English regularly and not merely spasmodically: of the year 994 the Chronicler says:–

> In this year came Olaf (Anlaf) and Svein to London, on the Nativity of St. Mary (Sept. 8th), with ninety four ships, and then they were obstinately fighting against the town, and would have set it on fire. But they there sustained more harm and evil than they ever weaned that any townsmen could do to them. For the holy mother of God, on that day, manifested her mercy to the townsmen, and delivered them from their foes. And they then went thence, and wrought the greatest evil that ever any army could do, in burning, and harrying, and in man-slayings, as well by the sea-coast, as in Essex, and in Kent, and in Sussex, and in Hampshire. And at last they took them horses, and rode as far as they would, and were doing unspeakable evil. Then the king and his "witan" resolved that they should be sent to, and promised tribute and food, provided that they should cease from ravaging; and they then accepted that. And all the army then came to Southampton, and there took winter-quarters; and there they were fed from all the realm of the West Saxons, and they were paid sixteen thousand pounds of money. Then the king sent bishop Aelfeah and the alderman Aethelweard after king Olaf; and the while hostages were given to the ships; and they then led Olaf with great worship to the king at Andover. And king Aethelred received him at the bishop's hand, and royally gifted him. And Olaf then promised him, as he also fulfilled, that he would never again come with hostility to England.

This Olaf was (afterwards, according to the sagas) King of Norway, and forced [Chris]tianity on his unwilling people: his history is one of the most splendid and dramatic chapters of the old Norse king-stories; but the incident has more significance as regards his fellow king Swein who was king of Denmark: he opens a new chapter in the story of the Norse invasions; the earlier ones though not altogether mere pillaging raids, since the Vikings had their wives and children, aimed rather at settlements than conquering of the whole kingdom: indeed there was then no kingdom to conquer, no centralized system of government, which as we have seen began to develop with Alfred: but now the struggle took the form of a definite attack by the Danish king on the English kingdom; which honey-combed by towns and settlements of his own blood was not hard to conquer: and also things to judge by the Chronicler were but in a poor way and the English tendency to muddle of which we have seen so much since was being well illustrated.

> An. DCCCC. XCIX. In this year the army again came about into the Thames, and then went up along the Medway, and to Rochester. And then the Kentish forces came against them, and they stoutly engaged together, but alas! that they too quickly gave way and fled; because they had not the support which they should have had. And the Danish had possession of the place of carnage; and then took horses and rode withersome they themselves would, and ruined and plundered almost all the West Kentish. Then the king with his "witen" resolved that they should be opposed with naval force, and also with a land force. But when the ships were ready, then they delayed from day to day, and harrassed the poor people who lay in the ships; and ever as it should be forwarder, so was it later, and from one time to another; and ever they let their foes' army increase, and ever they receded from the sea, and ever they went forth after them. And then in the end neither the naval force nor the land force was productive of anything but the people's distress, and a waste of money, and the emboldening of their foes.

The attempt at getting quit of the invaders by slaying all the Danes throughout England bettered matters little if at all: as the Chronicler laments they did not either pay or fight in time. In the year 1013 Swein had conquered England; and though he died soon after and his son Cnut had still a good deal of fighting to do, he soon became sole king of England.

So fell the country unto foreign kings; but the manners, laws and language of the two peoples were so much alike, that, the fighting once over, the social condition of the people was little altered and all would have gone smoothly if things could have remained thus. But England began more and more to be drawn into the European whirlpool.

There had for long been a regular intercourse with Rome; there was a School of the English there, and the Archbishop of

Canterbury had to fetch his pallium thence i.e. his investiture by
the Pope. The art of the English also was necessarily under
foreign influence: it was they who wedded to the strange inter-
lacing ornament which the Irish developed from the natural
growth of the soil and which had no power of giving even hints
at the human form, the figure drawing deduced from the art of
Byzantium, but which the English probably took from the
Germans who had an art which was an offshoot of the Byzantine
style: of the architecture of the English before the Conquest
there are but few specimens left: probably because their churches
were small for important places, and got rebuilt there in
succeeding ages: while in unimportant places they were built of
timber as the ordinary houses were and so perished by lapse of
time where they were not burned down or rebuilt. Scanty
however as the materials for judging of the architecture are they
are enough to tell us that the English had developed a style of
their own quite different from that which the Norman Conquest
introduced: the difference of the styles is the more marked as
there is at least one Norman church in England built before the
Conquest, Waltham Abbey, and one or two Saxon ones built after
it. I should mention that to my mind the Saxon[s] took their
architecture from the German version of the Byzantine style: all
things thus tending towards connecting England with the
Continent, it was not long before the great event came which
made England merely a part of the dominions of a French Duke.

Passing matters helped this forward: for Edward the
Confessor rested on the foreign element as a support against the
power of Earl Godwin and his sons; and gave a kind of a title to
the kingdom to Duke William: discontent grew; a riot at Dover
made by the French favourites was taken up by the Earl as an
occasion to appeal to the people against the King: he sailed up the
Thames to Southwark and lay there a tide, and shot the bridge
with the flood: the king's men were drawn up to receive him on
the Middlesex shore; and a great battle seemed imminent, but

the hearts of all men misgave them that they should fight Englishmen against Englishmen; truce was struck, the witan met, and Earl Godwin was reinstated in his lands and earldom with the good-will of all men; the evil customs and laws of the foreigners were done away with, and all looked hopeful. I have mentioned this passage about Godwin to show that the Danish blood was by this time scarcely looked on as alien, since Godwin the popular hero and supporter of the English customs was in fact a Northman.

Well Edward died amidst these things, but a little after Godwin and who but Godwin's son could be king after him; so Harald, called says one chronicler Harald the Hapless on his tombstone, became the last king of Early England. I have said that a[n] English History is apt to lack romance; yet the history of the great change for good and for evil which connected England forever with the continent could scarcely be more romantic. And here above all times does one regret that subjection of the native writers to monkish Latin, and longs for the story now never to be written which the English sagaman might have given us of that field of Hastings. And this all the more as one part of the story and that the least important part has been told dramatically enough by an Icelander. For Tostig Harald's brother having quarrelled with him and being dispossessed in consequence, sailed away north and tried to get Swein the Dane-king to fall on England; and getting the cold shoulder from him went to Harald the Terrible, king of Norway, a redoubted warrior, once captain of the guard of the Greek emperor, whom he enticed into the expedition: the story teller gives us all the usual preliminaries of a great tragedy in the tales of the north; pithy warnings of wise men; omens of seers, and the like; and dwells at length on the victories won by the Norse Harald before the English king caught him unawares, his army without their mail coats six miles from York: the fight that follows and the parley before it are given in the usual dramatic and generous manner of the north, and makes one long that such a story teller should have told us what followed. The news of Duke William's landing on Michaelmas-day; the hasty march south of King Harald and his house-carls, and his muster of an army at the 'Hoar Apple-tree'; the wedge array drawn up round the king and his brothers round the Banner of the fighting-man: the oft repulsed charges of French Horsemen; the breaking up of the wedge-array in pursuit, and the battle lost but the men still fighting; the arrow shot at a venture and the death of Harald and his brethren and England lost and won once more. All this was worthy of being told in more words than the brief despair of the Chronicler, and in more life-like manner than the Latin scribbling Monk could compass.

So England fell, and it seems that the people of the country were not at first conscious of what had happened; but thought of it as they would of the last fight of Cnut with Edmund Ironside, which simply put a Danish king over them instead of an English one without changing their social condition: you must remember that though there was more national feeling then than later on under the Plantegenets still there was but little. The national patriotism we are so noisy about now was born much later when the Middle Ages were ending.

What had happened was serious enough: England had fallen into the hands of a Romanized landlord and from henceforth was a part of the great European Feudal System: its development as a pure branch of the Teutonic family was stopped forever; because the countries to whom it was now to be bound were, whatever their blood was, developed from Roman provincials, and had not even a language of their own, but were compelled to speak a dialect of Latin.

What might else have happened in the social and political development of England, if the Frenchmen had been driven out by Harald, who can say. For my part I doubt if the difference would have been great. In the next two hundred years the real popular history of Europe is comprised in that of the guilds, which after a long struggle established their control over all industry, yet in the end too late to prevent their falling in their turn under the double curse of bureaucracy and commercialism, which grew to be ruling powers as feudalism or the society of status waned into capitalism or the society of contract. In this history England took a fair share, and could hardly have done otherwise considering her position and importance, even had there been no Duke William and no Hastings; and in these matters England remained England at all events—with her art and literature it is different. She almost immediately received a new architecture, which developing slight differences nevertheless clung close to that of France, and produced such glorious and beautiful [buildings] that there is no room for regret left— literature also became Frenchified and here to its great misfortune as I think. The great works of the English poets ever since Chaucer's time have had to be written in what is little more than a dialect of French and I cannot help looking on that as a mishap. If we could only have preserved our language as the Germans have theirs, I think we with our mingled blood would have made the world richer than it is now—but these are vain regrets: it is all whistled down the wind with the last shout of the axes at Senlac: nor do I ask you to look on it now except as on a series of pictures of the past.

This was what the axes of Hastings resisted had they known it: but if they had, and whatever resistance had been attempted the result would have been the same. The day of centralization and bureaucracy had to be prepared for: the remains of the tribal custom of the English supported by a loose approximation to the Romanized feudality made our forefathers too weak to resist the shadow of Rome now rising again from the dead in the wrappings of feudality. Moreover stout-hearted and valiant as they were they seem to have had a good share of that stupid wastefulness of which many Englishmen are still proud: to burn

the house down that our Sunday's beef may be cooked; to lose
ten men in a battle where one would be enough; in fine to
reduce ten counties to the condition of filthy cinder-heaps in
order that ten thousand men may have ten thousand a year each
(at other people's expense in all ways) this is the sort of wastefulness which we have grown fools enough to be proud of, but
which the old Saxon Chronicler lamented, not without reason:
since surely it was one of the causes that made the brilliant
victory at Stamford Bridge of no account; that broke the wedge-
array at Hastings, and laid Harald the Hapless the last king of
the English in a forgotten grave at Waltham Abbey amidst the
streams of Lea River.

FEUDAL ENGLAND

1887

The Norman Conquest found a certain kind of feudality in existence in England; a feudality which was developed from the customs of the tribes with little or no admixture of Roman law; and also even before the Conquest this country was slowly beginning to be mixed up with the affairs of the Continent of Europe, and that not only with the kindred nations of Scandinavia, but with the Romanised countries also. But the Conquest of Duke William did introduce the complete or Romanised Feudal system into the country; and it also connected it by strong bonds to the Romanised countries, but thereby laid the first foundations of national feeling in England. The English felt their kinship with the Norsemen or the Danes, and did not feel their conquests when they had become complete, and consequently mere immediate violence had disappeared from them; their feeling was tribal rather than national; but they could have no sense of co-nationality with the varied populations of the provinces which mere dynastical events had strung together into the dominion, the manor, one may say, of the foreign princes of Normandy and Anjou; and as the kings who ruled them gradually got pushed out of their French possessions, England became conscious of her separate nationality, though still only in a fashion, as the manor of an *English* lord.

It is beyond the scope of this article to give anything like a connected story, even of the slightest, of the course of events

between the conquest of Duke William and the fully developed
mediæval period of the 14th century, which is the England that I
have before my eyes as Mediæval. That period of the 14th
century united the developments of the elements which had
been stirring in Europe since the final fall of the Roman Empire,
and England shared in the general feeling and spirit of the age,
although from its position the course of its history, and to a
certain extent the lives of its people was different. It is to this
period, therefore, that I wish in the long run to call your
attention, and I will only say so much about the earlier period as
may be necessary to explain how the people of England got into
the position in which they were found by the statute of labourers
enacted by Edward III., and the Peasant's Rebellion in the time
of his grandson and successor Richard II.

Undoubtedly, then, the Norman Conquest made a complete
break in the continuity of the history of England. When the
Londoners after the Battle of Hastings accepted Duke William
for their king, no doubt they thought of him as being much in
the same position that the newly slain Harold had been; or at any
rate such a king as Knut the Dane, who had also conquered
England; and probably William himself thought no otherwise,
but the event was quite different, for on the one hand not only
was he a man of great character, able, masterful, and a great
soldier in the modern sense of the word, but he had at his back
his wealthy dukedom of Normandy, which he had himself
reduced to obedience and organised; and, on the other hand,
England lay before him, unorganised, yet stubbornly rebellious
to him; its very disorganisation and want of a centre making it
more difficult to deal with by merely over-running it with an
army levied for that purpose, and backed by a body of house-
carles or guards, which would have been the method of a
Scandinavian or native king in dealing with his rebellious
subjects. Duke William's necessities and instincts combined led
him into a very different course of action, which determined the

future destiny of the country. What he did was to quarter upon England an army of feudal vassals drawn from his obedient dukedom, and to hand over to them the lordship of the land of England in return for their military service to him, the suzerain of them all. Thenceforward, it was under the rule of these foreign landlords that the people of England had to develope.

The development of the country as a Teutonic people was checked and turned aside by this event. Duke William brought, in fact, his Normandy into England, which was thereby changed from a Teutonic people (theod) with the old tribal customary law still in use among them, into a province of Romanised Feudal Europe, a piece of France in short; and though in time she did grow into another England again, she missed for ever in her language, her literature, and her laws, the chance of developing into a great homogeneous Teutonic people infused usefully with a mixture of Celtic blood.

However, this step which Duke William was forced to take, further influenced the future of the country by creating the great order of the baronage, and the history of the early period of England is pretty much that of the struggle of the king with the baronage and the church. For William fixed the type of the successful English mediæval king, of whom Henry II. and Edward I. were also notable examples. It was, in fact, with him that the struggle towards monarchical bureaucracy began, which was checked by the barons, who extorted Magna Charta from King John, and afterwards by the revolt headed by Simon de Montfort in Henry III.'s reign; was carried on vigorously by Edward I., and finally successfully finished by Henry VII. after the long faction-fight of the Wars of the Roses, had weakened the feudal lords so much that they could no longer assert themselves against the monarchy.

As to the contest between the Crown and the Church, two things are to be noted; first, that at least in the earlier period the Church was on the popular side. Thomas Beckett was canonised, it is true, formally and by regular decree; but his memory was held so dear by the people that he would probably have been canonized informally by them if the holy seat at Rome had refused to do so. The second thing to be noted about the dispute is this, that it was no contest of principle. According to the mediæval theory of life and religion, the Church and the State were one: separate manifestations of the Kingdom of God upon earth which was part of the Kingdom of God in heaven; the king was an officer of that realm and a liegeman of God. The doctor of laws and the doctor of physic partook in a degree of the priestly character. On the other hand the Church was not withdrawn from the everyday life of men; the division into a worldly and spiritual life neither of which had much to do with the other, was a creation of the protestantism of the Reformation, and had no place in the practice at least of the mediæval Church, which we cannot too carefully remember is little more represented by modern Catholicism than by modern Protestantism. The contest, therefore, between the Crown and the Church was a mere bickering between two bodies, without any essential antagonism between them as to how far the administration of either reached: neither dreamed of subordinating one to the other, far less of extinguishing one by the other.

The history of the Crusades, by the way, illustrates very emphatically this position of the Church in the Middle Ages. The foundation of that strange feudal kingdom of Jerusalem, whose king had precedence in virtue of his place as lord of the centre of Christianity over all other kings and princes; the orders of men-at-arms vowed to poverty and chastity, like the Templars and Knights of St. John; and above all the unquestioning sense of duty that urged men of all classes and kinds into the holy war, show how strongly the idea of God's kingdom on the earth had taken hold of all men's minds in the early Middle Ages. As to the result of the Crusades, they certainly had their influence on the solidification of Europe and the great feudal system, at the head of which, in theory at least, were the Pope and the Kaiser. Doubt-less, also, the intercourse with the East gave Europe an oppor-tunity of sharing in the mechanical civilisation of the peoples originally dominated by the Arabs, and infused by the art of Byzantium and Persia, not without some tincture of the culti-vation of the later classical period.

The stir and movement also of the Crusades, and the neces-sities in which they involved the princes and their barons, furthered the upward movement of the classes that lay below the feudal vassals, great and little; the principal opportunity for which movement, however, in England, was given by the continuous struggle between the Crown and the Church and Baronage.

The early Norman kings, even immediately after the death of the Conqueror, found themselves involved in this struggle, and were forced to avail themselves of the help of what had now become the inferior tribe—the native English, to wit. Henry I., an able and ambitious man, understood this so clearly that he made a distinct bid for the favour of the inferior tribe by marrying an English princess; and it was by means of the help of his English subjects that he conquered his Norman subjects, and the field of Tenchebray, which put the coping-stone on his success, was felt by the English people as an English victory over the oppressing tribe with which Duke William had overwhelmed the English people. It was during the king's reign and under these influences that the trading and industrial classes began to rise somewhat. The merchant gilds (of which subject of gilds more hereafter) were now in their period of greatest power, and had hardly begun, as they did later, to develope into the corpora-tions of the towns; but the towns themselves were beginning to gain their freedom and to become an important element in the society of the time, as little by little they asserted themselves against the arbitrary rule of the feudal lords, lay or ecclesiastical: for as to the latter, it must be remembered that the Church included in herself the orders or classes into which lay society was divided, and while by its lower clergy of the parishes and (afterwards) by the friars it touched the people, its upper clergy were simply feudal lords; and as the religious fervour of the "cultivated clergy," which was marked enough in the earlier period of the Middle Ages (in Anselm, for example), faded out, they became more and more mere landlords, although from the conditions of their landlordism, living as they did on their land and amidst of their tenants, less oppressive than the lay landlords.

The order and progress of Henry I.'s reign, which marks the transition from the mere military camp of the Conqueror to the Mediæval England I have to dwell upon, was followed by the period of mere confusion and misery which accompanied the accession of the princes of Anjou to the throne of England. In this period the barons widely became mere violent and illegal robbers; and the castles with which the land was dotted, and which were begun under the auspices of the Conqueror as military posts, became mere dens of strong thieves. No doubt this made the business of the next able king, Henry II., the easier. He was a staunch man of business, and turned himself with his whole soul towards the establishment of order and the consolidation of the monarchy, which accordingly took a great stride under him towards its ultimate goal of bureaucracy. He would probably have carried the business still further, since in his contest with the Church, in spite of the canonisation of Beckett and the king's formal penance at his tomb, he had really gained a victory for the Crown, which it never really lost again; but in his days England was only a part of the vast dominion of his house, which included more than half of France, and his struggle with his feudatories and the French king, which sowed the seed of the loss of that dominion to the English Crown, took up much of his life and finally beat him. His two immediate successors, Richard I. and John, were good specimens of the chiefs of their line, almost all of whom were very able men, having even a touch of genius in them, but therewithal were such wanton blackguards and scoundrels that one is almost forced to apply the theological word "wickedness" to them. Such characters belong specially to their times, fertile as they were both of great qualities and of scoundrelism, and in which our own special vice of hypocrisy was entirely lacking. John, the second of these two pests, put the coping-stone on the villiany of his family, and lost his French dominion in the lump. Under such rascals as these came the turn of the baronage, and they, led by Stephen Langton, the archbishop who had been forced on the unwilling king by the Pope, united together and forced from him his assent to Magna-charta, the great, thoroughly well-considered deed, which is conventionally called the foundation of English Liberty, but which can only claim to be so on the ground that it was the confirmation and seal of the complete feudal system in England, and put the relations between the vassals, the great feudatories, and the king, on a stable basis, since it created or at least confirmed order among these privileged classes, among whom indeed it recognised the towns to a certain extent as part of the great feudal hierarchy: they had begun to acquire status in that hierarchy.

So John passed away, and became not long after an almost mythical personage, the type of the bad king. There are still ballads and prose stories of these in existence, which tell the tale of this strange monster as the English people imagined it. As they belong to the fourteenth century, the period I have undertaken to tell you about specially, I will give you one of these concerning the death of King John, for whom the people inagined a more dramatic cause of death than mere indigestion, of which in all probability he really died; and you may take it for a specimen of popular literature of the fourteenth century. I can make bold to quote from memory, since the quaint wording of the original, and the spirit of bold and blunt heroism which it breathes, have fixed it in my mind for ever. The King, you must remember, had halted at Swinestead Abbey in Lincolnshire in his retreat from

the hostile barons, and their French allies, and had lost all his
baggage by the surprsie of the advancing tide in the Wash; so that
he might well be in a somewhat sour mood. Says the tale: "So the
King went to meat in the hall, and before him was a loaf, and he
looked grimly on it and said, 'For how much is such a loaf sold
in this realm?' 'Sir, for one penny,' said they. Then the King
smote the board with his fist and said, 'By God, if I live for one
year such a loaf shall be sold for twelve pence!' That heard one
of the monks who stood thereby, and he thought and considered
that his hour and time to die was come, and that it would be a
good deed to slay so cruel a king and so evil a lord. So he went
into the garden and plucked plums and took out of them the
steles [stalks], and did venom in them each one; and he came
before the King and sat on his knee, and said: 'Sir, by St Austin,
this is the fruit of our garden.' Then the King looked evilly on
him and said, 'Assay them, monk!' So the monk took and ate
thereof, nor changed countenace any whit: so the King ate there-
after. But presently afterwards the monk swelled and turned
blue, and fell down and died before the King: then waxed the
King sick at heart, and he also swelled and died, and so he ended
his days."

For a while after the death of John and accession of Henry III.
the baronage, strengthened by the great Charter and with a weak
and wayward king on the throne, made their step forward in
power and popularity, and the first serious check to the tendency
to monarchical bureaucracy, a kind of elementary aristocratic
constitution, was imposed upon the weakness of Henry III.
Under this movement of the barons, who in their turn had to
seek for the support of the people, the towns made a fresh step
in advance, and Simon de Montfort, the leader of what for want
of a better word must be called the popular party, was forced by
his circumstances to summon to his parliament citizens from the
boroughs. Earl Simon was one of those men that come to the
front in violent times, and he added real nobility of character to

strength of will and persistence. He became the hero of the people, who went near to canonising him after his death. But the monarchy was too strong for him and his really advanced projects, which by no means squared with the hopes of the baronage in general; and when Prince Edward, afterwards Edward I., grown to his full mental stature, came to the help of the Crown with his unscrupulous business ability, the struggle was soon over; and with Evesham field the monarchy began to take a new stride, and the longest yet taken, towards bureaucracy.

Edward I. is remembered by us chiefly for the struggle he carried on with the Scotch baronage for the feudal suzerainty of that kingdom, and the centuries of animosity between the two kingdoms which that struggle drew on. But he has other claims to our attention besides this. At first, and remembering the ruthlessness of many of his acts, especially in the Scotch war, one is apt to look upon him as a somewhat pedantic tyrant and a good soldier, with something like a dash of hypocrisy beyond his time added. But, like the Angevine Kings I was speaking of just now, he was a completely characteristic product of his time. He was not a hypocrite probably, after all, in spite of his tears shed after he had irretrievably lost a game, or won one by stern cruelty. There was a dash of real romance in him, which mingled curiously with certain lawyer-like qualities. He was, perhaps, the man of all men who represented most completely the finished feudal system, and who took it most to heart. His law, his romance, and his religion, his self-command, and his terrible fury were all a part of this innate feudalism, and exercised within its limits; and we must suppose that he thoroughly felt his responsibility as the chief of his feudatories, while at the same time he had no idea of his having any responsibilities towards the lower part of his subjects. Such a man was specially suited to carrying on the tendency to bureaucratic centralisation, which culminated in the Tudor monarchy. He had his struggle with the baronage, but hard as it was he was sure not to carry it beyond

the due limits of feudalism; to that he was always loyal. He had
slain Earl Simon before he was king, while he was but his father's
general; but Earl Simon's work did not die with him, and hence-
forward while the Middle Ages and their feudal hierarchy lasted,
it was impossible for either king or barons to do anything
which would seriously injure each other's position; the struggle
ended in his reign in a balance of power in England which, on
the one hand, prevented any great feudatory becoming a rival of
the king, as happened in several instances in France, and on
the other hand prevented the king lapsing into a mere despotic
monarch. I have said that bureaucracy took a great stride in
Edward's reign, but it reached its limits under feudalism as far as
the nobles were concerned. Peace and order was established
between the different powers of the governing classes; hence-
forward, the struggle is between them and the governed; that
struggle was now to become obvious; the lower tribe was rising
in importance, becoming richer for fleecing, but also it was
beginning to have some power; this led the king first, and
afterward the barons, to attack it definitely; it was rich enough to
pay for the trouble of being robbed, and not yet strong enough
to defend itelf with open success, although the slower and less
showy success of growth did not fail it. The instrument of attack
in the hands of the barons was the ordinary feudal privilege, the
logical carrying out of serfdom; but this attack took place two
reigns later. We shall come to that further on. The attack on the
lower tribe now growing into importance in this reign was made
by the king; and his instrument was—Parliament.

I have told you that Simon de Montfort made some attempt
to get the burgesses to sit in his Parliament, but it was left to
Edward I. to lay the foundations firmly of Parliamentary representation, which he used for the purpose of augmenting the
power of the Crown and crushing the rising liberty of the towns,
though of course his direct aim was simply at—money.

The Great Council of the Realm was purely feudal; it was

composed of the feudatories of the king, theoretically of all of them, practically of the great ones only. It was, in fact, the council of the conquering tribe with their chief at their head; the matters of the due feudal tribute, aids, reliefs, fines, sentage, and the like—in short, the king's revenue due from his men—were settled in this council at once and in the lump. But the inferior tribe, though not represented there, existed, and, as aforesaid, was growing rich, and the king had to get their money out of their purses directly; which as they were not represented at the Council, he had to do by means of his officers (the sheriffs) dealing with them one after another, which was a troublesome job; for the men were stiff-necked and quite disinclined to part with their money; and the robbery having to be done on the spot, so to say, encountered all sorts of opposition, and, in fact, it was the money needs both of baron, bishop, and king which had been the chief instrument in furthering the progress of the towns. The towns would be pressed by their lords, king, or baron, or bishop, as it might be, and they would see their advantage and strike a bargain. For you are not to imagine that because there was a deal of violence going on in those times there was no respect for law; on the contrary, there was a quite exaggerated respect for it if it came within the four corners of the feudal feeling, and the result of this feeling of respect was the constant struggle for *status* on the part of the townships and other associations throughout the Middle Ages. Well, the burghers would say, "'Tis hard to pay this money, but we will put ourselves out to pay it if you will do something for us in return; let, for example, our men be tried in our own court, and the verdict be of one of compurgation instead of wager of battle," and so forth, and so forth. Well, all this sort of detailed bargaining was, in fact, a safeguard for the local liberties, so far as they went, of the towns and shires, and did not suit the king's views of law and order at all; and so began the custom of the sheriff (the king's officer, who had taken the place of the earl of the Anglo-Saxon

period) summoning the burgesses to the council, which
burgesses you must understand were not elected at the folkmotes
of the town, or hundred (of which more hereafter), but in a sort
of hole-and-corner way by a few of the bigger men of the place.
What the king practically said was this: "I want your money, and
I cannot be for ever wrangling with you stubborn churles at
home there, and listening to all your stories of how poor you are
and what you want; no, I want you to be *represented*. Send me up
from each one of your communes a man or two whom I can
bully or cajole or bribe to sign away your substance for you."

Under these circumstances it is no wonder that the towns
were not very eager in the cause of *representation*. It was no easy
job to get them to come up to London merely to consult as to the
kind of sauce with which they were to be eaten. However, they
did come in some numbers, and by the year 1295 something like
a shadow of our present Parliament was on foot. Nor need there
be much more said about this institution; as time went on its
functions got gradually extended by the petition for the redress
of grievances accompanying the granting of money, but it was
generally to be reckoned on as subservient to the will of the king,
who down to the late Tudor period played some very queer tunes
on this constitutional instrument.

Edward I. gave place to his son, who again was of the type of
king who had hitherto given the opportunity to the barons for
their turn of advancement in the constitutional struggle; and in
earlier times no doubt they would have taken full advantage of
the circumstances; as it was they had little to gain. The king did
his best to throw off the restraint of the feudal constitution, and
to govern simply as an absolute monarch. After a time of
apparent success he failed, of course, and only succeeded in
confirming the legal rights of feudalism by bringing about his
own formal deposition at the hands of the baronage, as a chief
who, having broken the compact with his feudatories, had necessarily forfeited his right. If we compare his case with that of

Charles I. we shall find this difference in it, besides the obvious one that Edward was held responsible to his feudatories and Charles towards the upper middle classes, the squirearchy, as represented by Parliament: that Charles was condemned by a law created for the purpose, so to say, and evolved from the principle of the representation of the propertied classes, while Edward's deposition was the real logical outcome of the confirmed feudal system, and was practically legal and regular.

The successor of the deposed king, the Third Edward, ushers in the complete and central period of the Middle Ages in England. The feudal system is complete: the life and spirit of the country has developed into a condition if not quite independent, yet quite forgetful, on the one hand of the ideas and customs of the Celtic and Teutonic tribes, and on the other of the authority of the Roman Empire. The Middle Ages have grown into manhood; that manhood has an art of its own, which, though developed step by step from that of Old Rome and New Rome, and embracing the strange mysticism and dreamy beauty of the East, has forgotten both its father and its mother, and stands alone triumphant, the loveliest, brightest, and gayest of all the creations of the human mind and hand. It has a literature of its own too, somewhat akin to its art, yet inferior to it, and lacking its unity, since there is a double stream in it. On the one hand, the Court poet, the gentleman, Chaucer, with his Italianising metre, and his formal recognition of the classical stories; on which, indeed, he builds a superstructure of the quaintest and most unadulterated mediævalism, as gay and bright as the architecture which his eyes beheld and his pen pictured for us, so clear, defined, and elegant; a sunny world even amidst its violence and passing troubles, like those of a happy child, the worst of them an amusement rather than a grief to the onlookers; a world that scarcely needed hope in its eager life of adventure and love, amidst the sunlit blossoming meadows, and green woods, and white begilded manor houses. A kindly and human muse is Chaucer's, nevertheless, interested in and amused by all life, but of her very nature devoid of strong aspirations for the future; and that all the more, since, though the strong devotion and fierce piety of the ruder Middle Ages had by this time waned, and the Church was more often lightly mocked than either feared or loved, still the *habit* of looking on this life as part of another yet remained: the world is fair and full of adventure; kind men and true and noble are in it to make one happy; fools also to laugh at, and rascals to be resisted, yet not wholly condemned; and when this world is over we shall still go on living in another which is a part of this picture. Note all, and be as merry as you may, never forgetting that you are alive and that it is good to live.

That is the spirit of Chaucer's poetry; but alongside of it existed yet the ballad poetry of the people, wholly untouched by courtly elegance and classical pedantry; rude in art but never coarse, true to the back-bone; instinct with indignation against wrong, and thereby expressing the hope that was in it; a protest of the poor against the rich, especially in those songs of the Foresters, which have been called the mediæval epic of revolt; no more gloomy than the gentleman's poetry, yet cheerful from courage, and not content. Half-a-dozen stanzas of it are worth a cart-load of the whining introspective lyrics of to-day; and he who, when he has mastered the slight differences of language from our own daily speech, is not moved by it, does not understand what true poetry means nor what its aim is.

There is a third element in the literature of this time which you may call Lollard poetry, the great example of which is William Langland's 'Piers Plowman.' It is no bad corrective to Chaucer, and in *form* at least belongs wholly to the popular side; but it seems to me to show symptoms of the spirit of the rising middle class, and casts before it the shadow of the new master that was coming forward for the workman's oppression. But I must leave what more I have to say on this subject of the art and literature of the fourteenth century for another occasion. In what I have just said, I only wanted to point out to you that the Middle Ages had by this time come to the fullest growth; and that they could give expression, which was all their own, to the ideas and life of the time. That time was in a sense brilliant and progressive, and the life of the worker was better than it ever had been, and might compare with advantage with what it became in after periods and with what it is now; and indeed, looking back upon it, there are some minds and some moods that cannot help regretting it, and are not particularly scared by the idea of its violence and lack of accurate knowledge of scientific details; but, however, one thing is clear to us now, the kind of thing which never is clear to most people living in such periods, namely, that whatever it was, it could not last but must change into something else.

The complete feudalism of the fourteenth century fell, as systems always fall, by its own corruption, by development of the seeds of change, some which indeed had lain asleep during centuries, to wake up into activity long after the events which had created them were forgotten.

The feudal system was naturally one of open war; and the alliances, marriages, and other dealings family with family, made by the kings and potentates, were always leading them into war by giving them legal claims, or at least claims that could be legally pleaded, to the domains of other lords, who took advantage of their being on the spot, of their strength in men or money, or their popularity with the baronage, to give immediate effect to their claims. Such a war was that by which Edward I. drew on England the enmity of the Scotch; and such again was the great war which Edward III. entered into with France. You must not suppose that there was anything in this war of a national, far less of a race character. The last series of wars before this time I am now speaking of in which race feeling counted for much was the Crusades. This French war, I say, was neither national, racial, or

tribal; it was the private business of a lord of the manor claiming
what he considered his legal rights of another lord who had, as
he thought, usurped them; and this claim his loyal feudatories
were bound to take up for him; loyalty to a feudal superior, not
patriotism to a country, was the virtue which Edward III.'s
soldiers had to offer if they had any call to be virtuous in that
respect. This war once started was hard to drop, partly because of
the success that Edward had, falling as he did on France with the
force of a country so much more homogeneous than it; and no
doubt it was a war very disastrous to both countries, and so may
be reckoned as amongst the causes which broke up the feudal
system. But the real causes lay much deeper than that. The
system was not capable of expansion in production; it was, in
fact, as long as its integrity remained untouched, an army fed by
slaves, who could not be properly and closely exploited; its free
men proper might do something else in their leisure, and so
produce art and literature, but their true business as members of
a conquering tribe, their concerted business, was to fight. There
was, indeed, a fringe of people between the serf and the free
noble who produced the matters of handicraft which were
needed for the latter, but deliberately, and as we should now
think, wastefully; and as these craftsmen and traders began to
grow into importance and to push themselves, as they could not
help doing, into the feudal hierarchy, as they acquired *status*, so
the sickness of the feudal system increased on it, and the shadow
of the coming commercialism fell upon it. That any set of people
who could claim to be other than the property of free men
should not have definite rights differentiated sharply from those
of other groups, was an idea that did not occur to the Middle
Ages; therefore, as soon as men came into existence that were not
serfs, and were not nobles, they had to struggle for *status* by
organising themselves into associations that should come to be
acknowledged members of the great feudal hierarchy; for indef-
inite and negative freedom was not allowed to any person in

those days; if you had not *status* you did not exist except as an outlaw. This is, briefly speaking, the motive power of necessity that lay behind the struggle of the town corporations and craft gilds to be free, a struggle which, though it was to result in the breaking up of the mediæval hierarchy, began by an appearance of strengthening it by adding to its members, increasing its power of production, and so making it more stable. About this struggle, and the kind of life which accompanied it, I may have to write another time, and so will not say more about it here. Except this, that it was much furthered by the change that gradually took place between the landlords and the class on whom all society rested, the serfs. These at first were men who had no more rights than chattel-slaves had, except that mostly, as part of the stock of the manor, they could not be sold off it; they had to do all the work of the manor, and to earn their own livelihood off it as they best could. But as the power of production increased, owing to better methods of working, and as the country got to be more settled, their task-work became easier of performance and their own land more productive to them; and that tendency to the definition and differentiation of rights, moreover, was at work for their benefit, and the custom of the manor defined what their services were, and they began to acquire rights. From that time they ceased to be pure serfs, and began to tend towards becoming tenants, at first paying purely and simply *service* for their holdings, but gradually commuting that service for fines and money payment—for rent, in short.

Towards the close of the fourteenth century, after the country had been depopulated by the Black Death, and impoverished by the long war, the feudal lords of these copyholders and tenants began to regret the slackness with which their predecessors had exploited their *property*, the serfs, and to consider that under the new commercial light which had begun to dawn upon them *they* could do it much better if they only had their property a little more in hand; but it was too late, for their property had acquired

rights, and therewithal had got strange visions into their heads of
a time much better than that in which they lived, when even
those rights should be supplanted by a condition of things in
which the assertion of rights for any one set of men should no
longer be needed, since all men should be free to enjoy the fruits
of their own labour. Of that came the great episode of the
Peasants' War, led by men like Wat Tyler, Jack Straw, and John
Ball, who indeed, with those they led, suffered for daring to be
before their time, for the revolt was put down with cruelty
worthy of an Irish landlord or a sweating capitalist of the present
day; but, nevertheless, serfdom came to an end in England, if not
because of the revolt, yet because of the events that made it, and
thereby a death-wound was inflicted on the feudal system. From
that time onward the country, passing through the various
toubles of a new French war of Henry Vth's time, and the War of
the Roses, did not heed these faction fights much. The workmen
grew in prosperity, but also they began to rise into a new class,
and form a class underneath the old working men, and to lay the
foundations of capitalistic production. England got carried into
the rising current of commercialism, and the rich men and
landlords to turn their attention to the production of profit
instead of the production of livelihood; the gildless journeyman
and the landless labourer slowly came into existence; the
landlord got rid of his tenants all he could, turned tillage into
pasture, and sweated the pastures to death in his eagerness for
wool, which for him meant money and the breeding of money;
till at last the place of the serf, which had stood empty, as it were,
during a certain transition period, during which the non-capital-
istic production was expanding up to its utmost limit, was filled
by the proletarian working for the service of a master in a new
fashion, a fashion which exploited and (woe worth the while!)
exploits him very much more completely than the customs of the
manor of the feudal period. I hope to be able hereafter to go into
the question of the life and production of the workman of the

earlier period. At present I will make an end by saying that the feudal serf worked hard, and lived poorly, and produced a rough livelihood for his master; whereas the modern workman, working harder still, and living little if any better than the serf, produces for his master a state of luxury of which the old lord of the manor never dreamed. The workman's powers of production are multiplied a thousandfold; his own livelihood remains pretty much where it was. The balance goes to his master and the crowd of useless, draggle-tailed knaves and fools who pander to his idiotic sham desires, and who, under the pretentious title of the intellectual part of the middle classes, have in their turn taken the place of the mediæval jester. Truly, if the Positivist motto, "Live for others," be taken in stark literality, the modern work-man should be a good and wise man, since he has no chance of living for himself! And yet, I wish he were wiser still; wise enough to make an end of the preaching of "Live *on* others," which is the motto set forth by commercialism to her favoured children.

Yet in one thing the modern proletarian has an advantage over the mediæval serf, and that advantage is a world in itself. Many a century lay between the serf and successful revolt, and though he tried it many a time and never lost heart, yet the coming change which his martyrdom helped on was not to be for him yet, but for the new masters of his successors. With us it is different. A few years of wearisome struggle against apathy and ignorance; a year or two of growing hope—and then who knows? Perhaps a few months, or perhaps a few days of the open struggle with brute force, with the mask off its face, and the sword in its hand, and then we are over the bar. Who knows, I say? Yet this we know, that ahead of us, with nothing betwixt except such incidents as are necessary to its development, lies the inevitable social revolution, which will bring about the end of mastery and the triumph of fellowship.

ART AND INDUSTRY IN THE FOURTEENTH CENTURY

1887

I n England, at least, if not on the Continent of Europe, there are some towns and cities which have indeed a name that recalls associations with the past, but have no other trace left them of the course of that history which has made them what they are. Besides these, there are many more which have but a trace or two left; sometimes, indeed, this link with the past is so beautiful and majestic in itself that it compels us when we come across it to forget for a few moments the life of to-day with which we are so familiar that we do not mark its wonders or its meannesses, its follies or its tragedies. It compels us to turn away from our life of habit which is all about us on our right hand and our left, and which therefore we cannot see, and forces on us the consideration of past times which we can picture to ourselves as a whole, rightly or wrongly, because they are so far off. Sometimes, as we have been passing through the shabby streets of ill-burnt bricks, we have come on one of these links with the past and wondered. Before the eyes of my mind is such a place now. You travel by railway, get to your dull hotel by night, get up in the morning and breakfast in company with one or two men of the usual middle-class types, who even as they drink their tea and eat their eggs and glance at the sheet of lies, inanity, and ignorance, called a newspaper, by their sides, are obviously doing

their business to come, in a vision. You go out into the street and
wander up it; all about the station, and stretching away to the left,
is a wilderness of small, dull houses built of a sickly-coloured
yellow brick pretending to look like stone, and not even able to
blush a faint brown blush at the imposture, and roofed with thin,
cold, purple-coloured slates. They cry out at you at the first
glance, workmen's houses; and a kind of instinct of information
whispers to you: railway workmen and engineers. Bright as the
spring morning is, a kind of sick feeling of hopeless disgust
comes over you, and you go on further, sure at any rate that you
cannot fare worse. The street betters a little as you go on;
shabbyish shops indeed, and mean houses of the bourgeoisie of a
dull market town, exhibiting in their shop fronts a show of goods
a trifle below the London standard, and looking "flash" at the
best; and above them dull houses, greyish and reddish, recalling
some associations of the stage-coach days and Mr. Pickwick and
Sam Weller, which would cheer you a little if you didn't see so
many gaps in their lines filled up with the sickly yellow-white
brick and blue slate, and with a sigh remember that even the
romance surrounding Mr. Winkle is fast vanishing from the
world. You let your eyes fall to the pavement and stop and stare
a little, revolving many things, at a green-grocer's shop whose
country produce probably comes mostly from Covent Garden,
but looks fresh and green as a relief from the jerry building.
Then you take a step or two onward and raise your eyes, and
stand transfixed with wonder, and a wave of pleasure and exulta-
tion sweeps away the memory of the squalidness of to-day and
the shabby primness of yesterday; such a feeling as takes hold of
the city-dweller when, after a night journey, he wakes and sees
through his windows some range of great and noble mountains.
And indeed this at the street's end is a mountain also; but
wrought by the hand and the brain of man, and bearing the
impress of his will and his aspirations; for there heaves itself up
above the meanness of the street and its petty commercialism a

mass of grey stone traceried and carved and moulded into a great triple portico beset with pinnacles and spires, so orderly in its intricacy, so elegant amidst its hugeness, that even without any thought of its history or meaning it fills your whole soul with satisfaction. You walk on a little and see before you at last an ancient gate that leads into the close of the great church, but as if dreading that when you come nearer you may find some piece of modern pettiness or incongruity which will mar it, you turn away down a cross street from which the huge front is no longer visible, though its image is still in your mind's eye. The street leads you in no long while to a slow-flowing river crossed by an ugly modern iron bridge, and you are presently out in the fields, and going down a long causeway with a hint of Roman work in it. It runs along the river through a dead flat of black, peaty-looking country where long rows of men and women are working with an overlooker near them, giving us uncomfortable suggestions of the land on the other side of the Atlantic as it was; and you half expect as you get near some of these groups to find them black and woolly haired; but they are white as we call it, burned and grimed to dirty brown though; fair-sized and strong-looking enough, both men and women; but the women rough-ened and spoilt, with no remains of gracefulness, or softness of face or figure; the men heavy and depressed-looking; all that are not young, bent and beaten, and twisted and starved and weathered out of shape; in short, English field-labourers. You turn your face away with a sigh toward the town again, and see towering over its mean houses and the sluggish river and the endless reclaimed fen the flank of that huge building, whose front you saw just now, plainer and severer than the front, but harmonious and majestic still. A long roof tops it and a low, square tower rises from its midst. The day is getting on now, and the wind setting from the north-west is driving the smoke from the railway-works round the long roof and besmirching it somewhat; but still it looks out over the huddle of houses and the black fen with its bent rows of potato-hoers, like some relic of another world. What does it mean? Over there the railway-works with their monotonous hideousness of dwelling-houses for the artisans; here the gangs of the field-labourers; twelve shillings a week for ever and ever, and the workhouse for all day of judgment, of rewards and punishments; on each side and all around the nineteenth century, and rising solemnly in the midst of it, that token of the "dark ages," their hope in the past, grown now a warning for our future.

A thousand years ago our forefathers called the place Mede-hamstead, the abode of the meadows. They used the Roman works and doubtless knew little who wrought them, as by the side of the river Nene they drew together some stockaded collec-tion of wooden and wattled houses. Then came the monks and built a church, which they dedicated to St. Peter; a much smaller and ruder building than that whose beauty has outlasted so many hundred years of waste and neglect and folly, but which seemed grand to them; so grand, that what for its building, what for the richness of its shrines, Medehamstead got to be called the Golden Burg. Doubtless that long stretching water there knew more than the monks' barges and the coracles of the fenmen, and the oars of the Norsemen have often beaten it white; but records of the sacking of the Golden Burg I have not got till the time when a valiant man of the country, in desperate contest with Duke William, the man of Blood and Iron of the day, led on the host of the Danes to those rich shrines, and between them they stripped the Golden Burg down to its stone and timber. Here-ward, that valiant man, was conquered and died, and what was left of the old tribal freedom of East England sank lower and lower into the Romanized feudality that crossed the Channel with the Frenchmen. But the country grew richer, and the craftsmen defter, and some three generations after that sacking of the Golden Burg, St. Peter's Church rose again, a great and noble pile, the most part of which we have seen to-day.

Time passed again; the feudal system had grown to its full height, and the cloud as big as a man's hand was rising up to overshadow it in the end. Doubtless this town played its part in this change: had a great gild changing to a commune, federating the craft-gilds under it; and was no longer called Medehamstead or the Golden Burg, but after its patron saint, Peterborough. And as a visible token of those times, the gilds built for the monks in the thirteenth century that wonderful piece of ordered beauty which you saw just now rising from out the grubby little streets of the early nineteenth century. They added to the great Church here and there in the fourteenth century, traceried windows to the aisles, two spirelets to the front, that low tower in the midst. The fifteenth century added certain fringes and trimmings, so to say, to the building; and so it was left to bear as best it could the successive waves of degradation, the blindness of middle-class puritanism, the brutality of the eighteenth-century squirearchy, and the stark idealless stupidity of the early nineteenth century; and there it stands now, with the foul sea of modern civilization washing against it; a token, as I said, of the hopes that were, and which civilization has destroyed. Might it but give a lesson to the hopes that are, and which shall some day destroy civilization!

For what was the world so utterly different from ours of this day, the world that completed the glories of the Golden Burg, which to-day is called Peterborough, and is chiefly known, I fear, as the depôt of the Great Northern Railway? This glorious building is a remnant of the feudal system, which even yet is not so well understood amongst us as it should be; and especially, people scarcely understand how great a gulf lies between the life of that day and the life of ours. The hypocrisy of so-called consti-tutional development has blinded us to the greatness of the change which has taken place; we use the words King, Parlia-ment, Commerce, and so on, as if their connotation was the same as in that past time. Let us very briefly see, for the sake of a better understanding of the art and industry embodied in such works as Peterborough Cathedral, what was the relation of the complete feudal system with its two tribes, the one the unproductive masters, the other the productive servants, to the older incomplete feudality which it superseded; or in other words, what the Middle Ages came to before the development of the seeds of decay in them became obvious.

On the surface, the change from the serf and baron society of the earlier Middle Ages to the later Gild and Parliament Middle Ages was brought about by the necessities of feudalism. The necessities of the conquering or unproductive tribe gave opportunities to the progressive part of the conquered or productive tribe to raise its head out of the mere serfdom which in earlier times had been all it could look to. At bottom, this process of the rise of the towns under feudalism was the result of economical causes. The poor remains of the old tribal liberties, the folk-motes, the meetings round the shire-oak, the trial by compurgation, all these customs which imply the equality of freemen, would have faded into mere symbols and traditions of the past if it had not been for the irrepressible life and labour of the people, of those who really did the work of society in the teeth of the arbitrary authority of the feudal hierarchy. For you must remember that its very arbitrariness made the latter helpless before the progress of the productive part of that society. The upper classes had not got hold of those material means of production which enable them now to make needs in order to satisfy them for the sake of profit; the miracle of the world-market had not yet been exhibited. Commerce, in our sense of the word, did not exist: people produced for their own consumption, and only exchanged the overplus of what they did not consume. A man would then sell the results of his labour in order to buy wherewithal to live upon or to live better; whereas at present he buys other people's labour in order to sell its results, that he may buy yet more labour, and so on to the end of the chapter; the mediæval man began with production, the modern begins with money. That is, there was no capital in our sense of the word; nay, it was a main care of the crafts, as we shall see later on, that there should be none. The money lent at usury was not lent for the purposes of production, but as spending-money for the proprietors of land: and their land was not capitalizable as it now is; they had to eat its produce from day to day, and used to travel about the country doing this like bands of an invading army, which was indeed what they were; but they could not, while the system lasted, drive their now tenants, erewhile serfs, off their lands, or fleece them beyond what the custom of the manor allowed, unless by sheer violence or illegal swindling; and also every free man had at least the use of some portion of the soil on which he was born. All this means that there was no profit to be made out of anything but the land; and profit out of that was confined to the lords of the soil, the superior tribe, the invading army, as represented in earlier times by Duke William and his hirelings. But even they could not accumulate their profit: the very serfdom that enabled them to live as an unproductive class forbade them to act as land capitalists: the serfs had to perform the customary services and nothing more, and thereby got a share of the produce over and above the economic rent, which surplus would to-day certainly not go to the cultivators of the soil. Now since all the class-robbery that there was was carried on by means of the land, and that not by any means closely or carefully, in spite of distinct arbitrary laws directed against the workers, which again were never fully carried out, it follows that it was easy for the productive class to live. Poor men's money was good, says one historian; necessaries were very cheap, that is, ordinary food (not the cagmag of to-day), ordinary clothing and housing; but luxuries were dear. Spices from the East, foreign fruits, cloth of gold, gold and silver plate, silk, velvet, Arras tapestries, Iceland gerfalcons, Turkish dogs, lions, and the like, doubtless cost far more than they do to-day. For the rest, men's desires keep pace with their power over nature, and in those days their desires were comparatively few; the upper class did not live so much more comfortably then than the lower; so there were not the same grounds or room for discontent as there are nowadays. A workman then might have liked to possess a canopy of cloth of gold or a big cupboard of plate; whereas now the contrast is no longer between splendour and simplicity, but between ease and anxiety, refinement and sordidness.

The ordinary life of the workman then was easy; what he suffered from was either the accidents of nature, which the society of the day had not yet learned to conquer, or the violence of his masters, the business of whose life was then open war, as it is now veiled war. Storm, plague, famine and battle, were his foes then; scarcity and the difficulty of bringing goods from one place to another were what pinched him, not as now, superabundance and the swiftness of carriage. Yet, in some respects even here, the contrast was not so violent as it is nowadays between rich and poor; for, if the artisan was apt to find himself in a besieged city, and had to battle at all adventure for his decent life and easy work, there were vicissitudes enough in the life of the lord also, and the great prince who sat in his hall like a god one day, surrounded by his gentlemen and men-at-arms, might find himself presently as the result of some luckless battle riding barefoot and bare-headed to the gallows-tree: distinguished politicians risked more then than they do now. A change of government was apt to take heads off shoulders.

What was briefly the process that led to this condition of things, a condition certainly not intended by the iron feudalism which aimed at embracing all life in its rigid grasp, and would not, if it had not been forced to it, have suffered the serf to escape from serfdom, the artisan to have any status except that of a serf, the gild to organize labour, or the town to become free? The necessities of the feudal lord were the opportunities of the towns: the former not being able to squeeze his serf-tenants beyond a certain point, and having no means of making his money grow,

had to keep paying for his main position by yielding up what he
thought he could spare of it to the producing classes. Of course,
that is clear enough to see in reading mediæval history; but what
gave the men of the towns the desire to sacrifice their hard
earnings for the sake of position, for the sake of obtaining a status
alongside that of the baron and the bishop? The answer to my
mind is clear: the spirit of association which had never died out
of the peoples of Europe, and which in Northern Europe at least
had been kept alive by the gilds which in turn it developed; the
strong organization that feudalism could not crush.

The tale of the origin and development of the gilds is as long
as it is interesting, and it can only be touched on here; for the
history of the gilds is practically the history of the people in the
Middle Ages, and what follows must be familiar to most of my
readers. And I must begin by saying that it was not, as some
would think (speaking always of Northern Europe), the towns
that made the gilds, but the gilds that made the towns. These
latter, you must remember once more, important as they grew to
be before the Middle Ages ended, did not start with being
organized centres of life political and intellectual, with tracts of
country whose business it was just to feed and nourish them; in
other words, they did not start with being mere second-rate
imitations of the Greek and Roman cities. They were simply
places on the face of the country where the population drawn
together by convenience was thicker than in the ordinary
country, a collection of neighbours associating themselves
together for the ordinary business of life, finding it convenient in
those disturbed times to palisade the houses and closes which
they inhabited and lived by. But even before this took place, and
while the unit of habitation was not even a village, but a home-
stead (or tun), our Teutonic and Scandinavian forefathers, while
yet heathens, were used to band themselves together for feasts
and sacrifices and for mutual defence and relief against accident
and violence into what would now be called benefit societies, but

which they called gilds. The change of religion from heathenism
to Christianity did not make any difference to these associations;
but as society grew firmer and more peaceful, as the commerce
of our forefathers became something more than the selling to
one town what the traders had plundered from another, these
gilds developed in one direction into associations for the defence
of the carriers and sellers of goods (who you must remember in
passing had little in common with our merchants and commercial people); and on the other side began to grow into associations for the regulation of the special crafts, amongst which the
building and clothing crafts were naturally pre-eminent. The
development of these two sides of the gilds went on together, but
at first the progress of the trading gilds, being administrative or
political, was more marked than that of the craft-gilds, and their
status was recognized much more readily by the princes of the
feudal hierarchy; though I should say once for all that the direct
development of the gilds did not flourish except in those
countries where the undercurrent of the customs of the free
tribes was too strong to be quite merged in the main stream of
Romanized feudality. Popes, bishops, emperors, and kings in
their early days fulminated against them; for instance, an association in Northern France for resistance to the Norse sea-robbers
was condemned under ferocious penalties. In England, at any
rate, where the king was always carrying on a struggle with his
baronage, he was generally glad to acknowledge the claims of the
towns or communes to a free administration as a make-weight to
the power of the great feudatories; and here as well as in
Flanders, Denmark, and North Germany, the merchant-gild was
ready to form that administrative power, and so slid insensibly
into the government of the growing towns under the name of the
Great Gild, the Porte, the Lineage, and so on. These Great Gilds,
the corporations of the towns, were from the first aristocratic and
exclusive, even to the extent of excluding manual workmen; in
the true spirit of Romanized feudalism, so diametrically opposed

to that of the earlier tribal communities, in the tales of which the great chiefs are shown smithying armour, building houses and ships, and sowing their fields, just as the heroes of the Iliad and the Odyssey do. They were also exclusive in another way, membership in them being in the main an hereditary privilege, and they became at last very harsh and oppressive. But these bodies, divorced from labour and being nothing but governors, or at most administrators, on the one hand, and on the other not being an integral portion of the true feudal hierarchy, could not long hold their own against the gilds of craft, who all this while were producing and organizing production. There was a continuous and fierce struggle between the aristocratic and democratic elements in the towns, and plenty of downright fighting, bitter and cruel enough after the fashion of the times; besides a gradual progress of the crafts in getting hold of the power in the communes or municipalities. This went on all through the thirteenth century, and in the early part of the fourteenth the artisans had everywhere succeeded, and the affairs of the towns were administered by the federated craft-gilds. This brings us to the culminating period of the Middle Ages, the period to which my remarks on the condition of labourers apply most completely; though you must remember that the spirit which finally won the victory for the craft-gilds had been at work from the first, contending not only against the mere tyranny and violence incidental to those rough times, but also against the hierarchical system, the essential spirit of feudality. The progress of the gilds, which from the first were social, was the form which the class-struggle took in the Middle Ages.

I will now try to go a little more in detail into the conditions of art and industry in those days, conditions which it is clear, even from the scattered hints given above, are very different from those of to-day; so different indeed, that many people cannot conceive of them. The rules of the crafts in the great towns of Flanders will give us as typical examples as can be got at; since the mechanical arts, especially of weaving, were there farther advanced than anywhere else in Northern Europe. Let us take then the cloth-weavers of Flanders, and see under what rules they worked. No master to employ more than three journeymen in his workshop: no one under any pretence to have more than one workshop: the wages fixed per day, and the number of hours also: no work to be done on holidays. If piecework (which was allowed), the price per yard fixed: but only so much and no more to be done in a day. No one allowed to buy wool privately, but at open sales duly announced. No mixing of wools allowed; the man who uses English wool (the best) not to have any others on his premises. English and other foreign cloth not allowed to be sold. Workmen not belonging to the commune not admitted unless hands fell short. Most of these rules and many others may be considered to have been made in the direct interest of the workmen. Now for safeguards for the public: the workman must prove that he knows his craft duly: he serves as an apprentice first, then as journeyman, after which he is a master if he can manage capital enough to set up three looms besides his own, which, of course, he generally could do. Width of web is settled; colour of list according to quality; no work to be done in a frost, or in a bad light. All cloth must be "walked" or fulled a certain time, and to a certain width; and so on, and so on. And finally every piece of cloth must stand the test of examination, and if it fall short, goes back to the maker, who is fined; if it come up to the due standard it is marked as satisfactory.

Now you will see that the accumulation of capital is impossible under such regulations as this, and it was meant to be impossible. The theory of industry among these communes was something like this. There is a certain demand for the goods which we can make, and a certain settled population to make them: if the goods are not thoroughly satisfactory we shall lose our market for them and be ruined: we must therefore keep up their quality to the utmost. Furthermore, the work to be done must be shared amongst the whole of those who can do it, who must be sure of work always as long as they are well behaved and industrious, and also must have a fair livelihood and plenty of leisure; as why should they not?

We shall find plenty of people to-day to cry out on this as slavery; but to begin with, history tells us that these workmen did not fight like slaves at any rate; and certainly a condition of slavery in which the slaves were well fed, and clothed, and housed, and had abundance of holidays, has not often been realized in the world's history. Yes, some will say, but their minds were enslaved. Were they? Their thoughts moved in the narrow circle maybe; and yet I can't say that a man is of slavish mind who is free to express his thoughts, such as they are; still less if he habitually expresses them; least of all if he expresses them in a definite form which gives pleasure to other people, what we call producing works of art; and these workmen of the communes did habitually produce works of art.

I have told you that the chief contrast between the upper and lower classes of those days was that the latter lacked the showy pomp and circumstance of life, and that the contrast rather lay there than in refinement and non-refinement. It is possible that some readers might judge from our own conditions that this lack involved the lack of art; but here, indeed, there was little cause for discontent on the part of the lower classes in those days; it was splendour rather than art in which they could feel any lack. It is, I know, so difficult to conceive of this nowadays that many people don't try to do so, but simply deny this fact; which is, however, undeniable by any one who had studied closely the art of the Middle Ages and its relation to the workers. I must say what I have often said before, that in those times there was no such thing as a piece of handicraft being ugly; that everything made had a due and befitting form; that most commonly, however ordinary its use might be, it was elaborately orna-mented; such ornament was always both beautiful and inventive, and the mind of the workman was allowed full play and freedom in producing it; and also that for such art there was no extra charge made; it was a matter of course that such and such things should be ornamented, and the ornament was given and not sold. And this condition of the ordinary handicrafts with reference to the arts was the foundation of all that nobility of beauty which we were considering in a building like Peterborough Cathedral, and without that its beauty would never have existed. As it was, it was no great task to rear a building that should fill men's minds with awe and admiration when people fell to doing so of set purpose, in days when every cup and plate and knife-handle was beautiful.

When I had the Golden Burg in my eye just now, it was by no means only on account of its external beauty that I was so impressed by it, and wanted my readers to share my admiration, but it was also on account of the history embodied in it. To me it and its like are tokens of the aspirations of the workers five centuries ago; aspirations of which time alone seemed to promise fulfilment, and which were definitely social in character. If the leading element of association in the life of the mediæval workman could have cleared itself of certain drawbacks, and have developed logically along the road that seemed to be leading it onward, it seems to me it could scarcely have stopped short of forming a true society founded on the equality of labour: the Middle Ages, so to say, saw the promised land of Socialism from afar, like the Israelites, and like them had to turn back again into the desert. For the workers of that time, like us, suffered heavily from their masters: the upper classes who lived on their labour, finding themselves barred from progress by their lack of relation to the productive part of society, and at the same time holding all political power, turned towards aggrandizing themselves by perpetual war and shuffling of the political positions, and so opened the door to the advance of bureaucracy, and the growth of that thrice-accursed spirit of nationality which so hampers us even now in all attempts towards the realization of a true society. Furthermore, the association of the time, instinct as it was with hopes of something better, was exclusive. The commune of the Middle Ages, like the classical city, was unhappily only too often at strife with its sisters, and so became a fitting instrument for the greedy noble or bureaucratic king to play on. The gildsman's duties were bounded on the one hand by the limits of his craft, and on the other by the boundaries of the liberties of his city or town. The instinct of union was there, otherwise the course of the progress of association would not have had the unity which it did have: but the means of intercourse were lacking, and men were forced to defend the interests of small bodies against all comers, even those whom they should have received as brothers.

But, after all, these were but tokens of the real causes that checked the development of the Middle Ages towards Communism; that development can be traced from the survival of the primitive Communism which yet lived in the early days of the Middle Ages. The birth of tradition, strong in instinct, was weak in knowledge, and depended for its existence on its checking the desire of mankind for knowledge and the conquest of material nature: its own success in developing the resources of labour ruined it; it opened chances to men of growing rich and powerful if they could succeed in breaking down the artificial restrictions imposed by the gilds for the sake of the welfare of their members. The temptation was too much for the craving ignorance of the times, that were yet not so ignorant as not to have an instinct of what boundless stores of knowledge lay before the bold adventurer. As the need for the social and political organization of Europe blotted out the religious feeling of the early Middle Ages which produced the Crusades, so the need for knowledge and the power over material nature swept away the communistic aspirations of the fourteenth century, and it was not long before people had forgotten that they had ever existed.

The world had to learn another lesson; it had to gain power, and not be able to use it; to gain riches, and starve upon them like Midas on his gold; to gain knowledge, and then have newspapers for its teachers; in a word, to be so eager to gather the results of the deeds of the life of man that it must forget the life of man itself. Whether the price of the lesson was worth the lesson we can scarcely tell yet; but one comfort is that we are fast getting perfect in it; we shall, at any rate, not have to begin at the beginning of it again. The hope of the renaissance of the time when Europe first opened its mouth wide to fill its belly with the east wind of commercialism, that hope is passing away, and the ancient hope of the workmen of Europe is coming to life again. Times troublous and rough enough we shall have, doubtless, but not that dull time over again during which labour lay hopeless and voiceless under the muddle of self-satisfied competition.

It is not so hard now to picture to oneself those grey masses of stone, which our forefathers raised in their hope, standing no longer lost and melancholy over the ghastly misery of the fields and the squalor of the towns, but smiling rather on their new-born sisters the houses and halls of the free citizens of the new Communes, and the garden-like fields about them where there will be labour still, but the labour of the happy people who have shaken off the curse of labour and kept its blessing only. Between the time when the hope of the workman disappeared in the fifteenth century and our own times, there is a great gap indeed, but we know now that it will be filled up before long, and that our own lives from day to day may help to fill it. That is no little thing and is well worth living for, whatever else may fail us.

THE DEVELOPMENT OF MODERN SOCIETY

1890

All the progressive races of man have gone through a stage of development during which society has been very different to what it is now. At present there is a very definite line of distinction drawn between the personal life of a man and his life as a member of society. As a rule, the only direction in which this social life is felt is in that of his nearest kindred—his wife, children, parents, brothers and sisters. This is so much the case that we to-day have given to the word *relations* (which should mean all those with whom a man has serious and continuous dealings) a fresh meaning, and made it signify only those near members of kinship aforesaid. For the rest most civilised men acknowledge no responsibility. Though the word State is in everybody's mouth, most people have but the vaguest idea as to what it means; it is even generally considered as a synonym to the Government, which also indicates either the heads of one of the political parties, or the vague entity called by Carlyle the parish constable—in other words, the executive power of the ruling classes in our society. So little do we feel any responsibilities to this hardly conceivable thing, the State, that while few indeed feel any loyalty towards it, most men do not realise it sufficiently even to feel any enmity against it—except, perhaps, when the tax-gatherer's hand is on the knocker.

Now all this is so far the result of a long series of history, which I must just hint at before one comes to the condition of the workman during its different stages,—a series of events which tended to give to the word *property* the meaning which it now has; a series of events which tended more and more to consider *things* as the important matter of consideration rather than *persons*; which I may illustrate by the fact that nowadays the law looks upon the *estate* as of more importance than the user of it, as for instance in the case of the estate of a lunatic, which it will defend to the utmost against all attacks, and treat as if it had a genuine life and soul capable of feeling all injuries and pains, while all the time the lunatic is under restraint.

I will now contrast this entire ignoring of the community (for that will be a better word than *State* to use at present) with the conditions under which men lived in earlier ages of the world, and through which, as I have said, all the progressive races have passed, some of them so early that when we first meet them in history they are already passing out of it into the next development. In this early period the individual is so far from feeling no responsibility to the community, that all his responsibilities have relation to the community. Indeed, this sense of responsibility, as we shall see later on, has only been completely extinguished since the introduction of the present economical and political system—since the death of feudality, in short: but in the period I am thinking about it was a quite unquestioned habit. The unit of society, the first, and in the beginning the only bond, was the narrowest form of clan, called the *gens*. This was an association of persons who were traceably of one blood or kinship. Inter-marriage between its members was forbidden, or rather was not even dreamed of: a man of the Eagle gens could have no sexual intercourse with an Eagle woman, nor thought of it. All property was in common within the gens, and descent was traced, not through the father, but through the mother, who was the obvious parent of the child. Whatever *competition* (war, you may call it, for

competition was simple in those days), was outside the group
of blood relations, each of which felt no responsibility for
other groups of their members. But the fact that intermarriage
was impossible within these groups brought about a larger
association. Since an Eagle could not marry an Eagle, the Eagles
must either get their wives by violent robbery in a haphazard
fashion from outsiders, or have some other society at hand into
which they could marry, and who could marry into their society.
It used to be thought that the violent robbery was the method,
but I believe the second method was the one used. There were
groups of neighbours at hand who were recognised as belonging
to the same stock, but who were not too near in blood to make
marriage impossible. Between these groups there was affinity,
therefore; the Eagles could intermarry with the Owls, the
Sparrows, the Cats, or what not, according to a somewhat intri-
cate system, and this quite without violence. And also between
the clans or gentes who composed these tribes there would be no
war, and the *use* of whatever land they fed their stock upon or
cultivated (for in some places or ages this gentile-tribal system
lasted well into the agricultural period) was arranged peaceably in
a communal method.

Now the tribe in which a common ancestor (worshipped as a
god) was always assumed, and was generally a fact, tended to
federate with other tribes who still felt that they belonged to a
common stock, who thus formed an association called by our
ancestors the *thiod*, or people; an association much looser, of
course, than that of the gens or tribe, but like those, founded on
an idea of common kindred; founded on the personal kinship of
all its members to the god-ancestor, and not on locality or the
holding of certain property or position. The offices of the body,
under whatever names they went, were appointed by the
tribesmen for their personal qualities to perform definite duties.
There was no central executive body; every freeman had certain
necessary duties to perform, a shadow of which still exists in our

jury, who were originally the neighbours called together to utter their finding (without direction from a judge) as to how such a one had come by his death, what was to do between two neighbours who could not agree, and so forth. If a man was injured, it was the duty of the members of his gens or clan to take up the injury as an injury to the community. This is the meaning of the blood-feud of which we hear so much in the early literature of the North, and of the Celtic clans, and a survival of which still exists among out-of-the-way folks. The practice of the vendetta in Corsica, *e.g.*, does not indicate that the Corsicans are a specially vindictive people; it is a survival of the tribal customary law: its sentimentalising by novelists and poets is a matter of ignorance—naturally enought, I admit. "Government" or administration, or whatever else you may call it, was in this condition of society as direct as it ever can be; nor had government by majority been invented—*e.g.*, if the clans could not agree to unite in war, the war could not go on, unless any clan chose to go to war by itself.

I am conscious of not explaining fully the difference between such a state of society and ours; but it is indeed difficult to do so now, when all our ideas and the language which expresses them have been for so many ages moulded by such a totally different society. But I must, at least, try to make you understand that the whole of the duties of a freeman in this society had reference to the community of which he formed a part, and that he had no interests but the interest of the community; the assertion of any such private interests would have been looked upon as a crime, or rather a monstrosity, hardly possible to understand. This feudal union of the tribes is the last state of society under barbarism; but before I go on to the next stage, I must connect it with our special subject, the condition of productive labour.

With the development of the clans into federated tribes came a condition of organised aggressive war, since all were recognised as enemies outside of the tribe or federation; and with this came

the question what was to be done with the prisoners taken in
battle, and, furthermore, what was to be done with the tribe
conquered so entirely as not to be able to defend its possessions,
the land, which it used. Chattel slavery was the answer to the one
question, serfdom to the second. You see this question was
bound to come up in some form, as soon as the productive
powers of man had grown to a certain point. The very early
stages of society slaves are of no use, because your slave will die
unless you allow him to consume all that he produces; it is only
when by means of tools and the organisation of labour that he
can produce more than is absolutely necessary for his livelihood,
that you can take anything from him. Robbery only begins when
property begins; so that slavery doesn't begin till tribes are past
the mere hunter period. When they go to war they only save
their prisoners to have some fun out of them by torturing them,
as the redskins did, unless, perhaps, as sometimes happened, they
adopt them into the tribe, which also the redskins did at times.
But in the pastoral stage slaves become possible, and when you
come to the agricultural stage (to say nothing of further developments) they become necessary till the time when privilege is
destroyed and all men are equal. There are, then, three conditions of mankind, mere gregarious organised savagery, slavery,
and social equality. When you once have come to that conclusion
you must also come to this deduction from it, that if you shrink
from any sacrifice to the Cause of Socialism it must be because
we are either weak or criminal, either cowards or tyrants—
perhaps both.

Well, this last stage of barbarism, that of the federated tribes,
gave way in ancient history, the history of the Greeks and
Romans, into the first stage of civilisation. The life of the city,
and in mediæval history into feudalism; it is under the latter that
the development of the treatment of the conquered tribe as serfs
is the most obvious; serfdom being the essence of mediæval
society proper, and its decay beginning with the decline of

serfdom. But, undoubtedly, there were serfs in the classical period; that is to say an inferior class to the freemen, who were allowed to get their own livelihood on the condition of their performing certain services for them, and with a certain status, though a low one, which raised them above the condition of the chattel-slave, whose position was not recognised at all more than that of his fellow labourer, the horse or the ass. The Helots, for example, were the serfs rather than the slaves of the Spartans, and there were other instances both among the Greeks and the Romans of labourers in a similar position.

However, chattel slavery as opposed to serfdom is the characteristic form of servitude in the ancient city life. In that life you must understand the idea of the merging of the individual into the community was still strong, although *property* had come into existence, and had created a political condition of society under which *things* were growing to be of more moment than *persons*. But the community had got to be an abstraction, and it was to that abstraction, and not to the real visible body of persons that individual interests were to be sacrificed. This is more obvious among the Romans than the Greeks, whose mental individuality was so strong and so various, that no system could restrain it; so that when that system began to press heavily upon them they could not bear it, and in their attempts to escape from its consequences fell into the mere corruption of competitive tyranny at an early period. The Romans, on the other hand, without art or literature, a hard and narrow-minded race, cultivated this worship of the city into an over-mastering passion, so fierce and so irrational that their history before their period of corruption reads more like that of a set of logical demons bent on torturing themselves and everybody else, than a history of human beings. They must be credited with the preservation of the art and literature of Greece (though with its corruptions and stultification as well), and for the rest I think the world owes them little but its curse, unless indeed we must accept them as a terrible example of over-organisation. Of their state one may say what one of their poets said of their individual citizens, when they were sunk in their well-earned degradation, that for the sake of life they cast away the reasons for living.

But further, you must not fail to remember that the aspirations and nobility of sacrifice of the ancient city life were for [a] limited class only. In the old tribal life the slaves were not an important class, and also had easements, and even a kind of position which we do not associate with slave life, scarcely even with serfdom; as one may see in Homer, who, writing at a time when the tribal society was rapidly merging into city-life, gives us, for example, such a picture of a slave as Eumœus, who had at any rate plenty of pigs to eat, and also had a slave of his own "bought with his own wealth." But as the power of production increased and commerce with it, such laziness and pieces of unthrift went out of fashion, and though when a slave was valuable as a grammarian, a schoolmaster, an astronomer, or what not, his position was not intolerable; yet the general condition of slaves is best indicated by such facts as that they could not contract marriage, their evidence in a law case could only be taken under torture, and so forth. Among the Romans the idea of slavery was understood according to the pitiless logic characteristic of that people, *e.g.*, the debtor when delivered over to his creditors as a slave, could be divided among them in the most literal manner; they could cut him up in pieces and carry away each his dividend to do what they pleased with.

The equality, therefore, of the classical period, that splendid ideal of equality of duties and rights, only applied to the freemen of the clan as in the earlier times; but, as aforesaid, those outside the pale of that equality were of much more importance than they had been. At first, both in Greece and Rome, a great deal of the field-work was done by the freemen; the family were only helped in it by the slaves. Also a great deal of the handicraft was done either by poor free citizens, who could not afford to possess slaves, or by the strangers (metœci), who had no political rights, but were nobody's property; though even then the great mass of production was performed by the man or woman out of the labour-market, in which the selling of a human being was more obvious than it is at present. But as society in general grew richer, and the occupations fell more and more under the division of labour system, slave labour increased very much, till in the last days of the Roman republic the proportions of slave to free labour relatively to the handicrafts and agriculture had quite changed. The land, the *ownership* of which had been common in the early days, and the *use* divided among the citizens, had now got into the hands of big and very big landlords, who cultivated them wholly by slave-labour, superintendence and all, the livelihood being doled out to these poor devils on strict commercial principles, such as regulate the feed of a horse or cow, or an English labouring man. The despair of men so treated shook the Roman State in one tremendous slave-mutiny, that of Spartacus, and tormented society for centuries in countless minor mutinies by sea and land, till in the novels of the later Greeco-Roman civilisation (which are doubtless mere imitations of earlier works), adventures with organised bands of brigands and pirates form the stock incidents of the tale.

All this had been developing from the hey-day of Greek civilisation, but it did not blossom fully till the rise and growth of a monied middle-class in Rome had exaggerated and confirmed all the evils that were sure to be born out of a system of privileged freemen, who as they got richer got idler and more corrupt, and chattel-slaves, who as their masters got more corrupt, lost more and more of the alleviations of their lot which they had in earlier times; probably because their masters worked with them and lived pretty hardly like themselves, and could feel that instinctive sympathy which fellowship in labour instils into a man. Indeed, that loose easy-going generosity, that good-nature, in a word, of which there are indications in the Homeric poems, and which is found in fuller measure though in a more brutal form in the old English Tory squire ideal, you must not expect to find in the highly cultivated Greek citizen, who was mostly a prig; or in the energetic public-spirited Roman, who was mainly a jailer.

By the time I have been speaking of, Roman civilised society had come to be composed in the main of a privileged class of very rich men, whose business was war, politics and pleasure; and money-making as an instrument of these enjoyments; of their hangers-on forming a vast parasitical army; of a huge population of miserable slaves; and of another population of free men (so-called) kept alive by doles of food, and contented with peoples palaces in the form of theatrical and gladiatorial shows. That is, the free citizen had become an idler, either a rich luxurious one, or a pauper, and the work was done by men under the most obvious form of compulsion.

Thus was classical society, founded on the corruption of the society of the tribes by the institution of private property, brought to a dead-lock, the history of which is indeed a dreary page of the world's story. Art and literature are not forgotten, not buried, but for want of courage and invention are allowed to walk about like galvanised corpses of what was once so gloriously alive. Virtue? Does it exist at all? In high places there is none of it, nay, not even a sense of the lack of it. Virtue is to be found only in such places as the ranks of wild sectaries, outcasts from society. Warlike heroism? Time was when Hannibal a conqueror beset the city, and the stout-hearted citizens coolly bought and sold the use of the land he encamped on, and the greatest general that the world has seen drew off hopeless. Time was again and a Gothic chief lay before Rome preparing for its storm, and *his* estimate of the valour of the Roman citizens when the envoys appealed to his prudence and asked him not to drive such a huge population to despair, was given in the words "The thicker the hay, the easier to mow." In short, virtue had been used for acquiring power and riches; the bargain had been made, the riches spent, and the virtue gone; nothing was left. So it has been, so it will be, while violence and greed are the foundations of prosperity.

Such was the result of the organisation of Rome. If the ancient civilisation had been alone in the world then, if there had been nothing strong and progressive outside the world of civilisation, as is now the case, what would have happened? Who can say? Probably a more complete break up than that which followed on the downfall of Rome. As it was the world was delivered from its deadlock by the advent of the tribes of the North and the East, who were, when the Romans first showed consciousness of them other than by meeting them in battle, as specially in the pages of Tacitus, in a condition not differing much from that of the Latins themselves when they first began to wall round the hills beside the Tiber. They were, in fact, in their later days of tribal society. The story of the way in which they over-run the empire and furnished fresh blood to its worn-out population is well known enough. I can only wish that we had the story as told by the conquerors to set beside the naturally querulous one of the conquered, who, of course, did not like the process of their being improved out of existence. The story would then have been less empty of local and individual interest than it is now. In any case, however, the broad facts remain, which resolve themselves at last in the foundation of the feudal system; which was, in the main, the development of the customs of the Celtic, Teutonic, and Gothic tribes, customs which differed little from each other, and not much from those of the classical peoples before their development of the city and its life. In all parts of Europe remote from the influence of Rome this development was simple and traceable enough, but where the Germanic and Celtic races took the place of the Roman dominion and colonies, it was natural enough that they should wear the dress, so to say, of the older institutions, which in many cases they never quite shook off, though in essence they were everywhere the same.

The Teutonic and Gothic invaders of the empire had not got to the stage of city life, and did in fact miss that stage altogether. The feudal system was based not on the city and its wards, urban and rural, as was the case in ancient society, but on the country district, the manor and its townships. When our Anglo-Saxon forefathers first conquered Romanised Britain, they did not know what to do with the cities they won; they let them lie in ruins, and went to live down the dales on the borders of the streams in their homesteads, just as their ancestors had done in the clearings of the great central forest of Europe.

In these country districts, both in England and elsewhere, they held for a long time to many of their old tribal customs; the jury of neighbours; frank-pledge, or the responsibility of the district for the conduct of its dwellers; the oath of compurgation; the courts in the open-air; the folk-motes of all the freemen meeting directly (not by delegates) and armed in token of their freedom. Over all this, which still existed in the beginning of feudalism, and never quite disappeared until its wane, the regular feudal system was super-imposed. Serfdom took the place of thralldom; the King and his house-carles, or private body-guard, gave way to the King the head of the conquering tribe, who was the vicegerent of God, and granted the holding of lands to his tribesmen on condition of service from them, many of whom in their turn granted lands to others on similar terms; the performance of certain duties or service in return for the undisturbed holding of land, and having in consequence a definite recognised position, being the essence of mediæval society. I may remark in passing that the theory of property is quite different from that of our own days, in which the holding of property has been changed into a definite ownership which has no duties attached to it.

Now, I ask you to understand that the attainment of position or status, was the one aspiration of those who were in an inferior position during the Middle Ages. Even the serfs, many of whom at first were not very distinguishable from mere chattel-slaves, gained status by becoming *adscripti glebæ*, men attached to the manor on which they lived, and under the protection of its lord, to whom they had to render certain definite services in return; and there was a tendency from quite early days for these serfs to raise their position by becoming tenants of the lord of the manor, and also by their individually getting themselves received into a free town, and so emancipating themselves from individual service. The mention of this last incident calls my attention to the other members of the mediæval hierarchy, the Free Towns and the Guilds, who lay between the two poles of the landed nobility and their serfs. And you must remember that though the development of these took place somewhat late in the Middle Ages, they were both of them in existence from its very first days, when the tribes first reconstituted society after the break-up of the Roman Empire. Indeed, the growth of the free towns resembled in many respects the growth of Rome in her first days. The germs of them were always the agricultural district, in-habited by such and such a clan or tribe, whose members in early days were, or professed to be, akin to each other by blood, and held at least their land in common. Now in such and such a case this clan of freemen would gather to some more convenient part of their hundred, or district, and would fence it to protect their houses and crafts, and so population would grow thicker there; and they would hold a market there, and attract to them traders and men who needed protection for their handicrafts, though these would mostly be people outside the clan, unfree men, taking no part in the administration of the place.

Thus there grew up gradually classes of privileged and un-privileged within the towns, the former being the corporations of them, who, as the feudal system grew, got their status recognised by the king or over-lord, and who little by little freed themselves from the services, tolls, and restrictions which the neighbouring military chief had managed to enmesh them in as they passed out of their tribal freedom into the feudal power. This freedom they principally bought from their feudal lord, for their production was always expanding, since they were in the main communities of workers; whereas the revenue of the lord could not expand much, as it depended on the services of his serfs, which were limited by the customs of his manors. Remember once for all, that capitalism was unknown in those days, and the nobles could not live by rack-rent and interest, which in these days procure them such enormous incomes. So the towns, as their production expanded, bought their privileges with money down, and began to grow wealthy and powerful, and therewithal the ruling bodies in them, the corporations, who now represented the freemen of the clan, began to be corrupt and oppressive. They were no longer workmen, but were grown into a municipal aristocracy, very exclusive and mainly heriditary. But at this point these were met by the other associations I have named, the Guilds, which had been growing up under them all this while.

I have said that the guilds existed from the earliest period of the Middle Ages. I might have gone further, and pointed out their analogy to the free towns in this respect that they were not unknown to classical antiquity. In the early days of Rome, and before the labour of the free artisan was swamped by the enormous flood of slave-labour, it flourished in that city. In fact, it seems to me that these guilds are an answer to the imperative claim for useful association which human nature makes; as one form of society which once served its purpose duly fails men, they are forced to form others, even while the old form exists and has become mere authority and an instrument of oppression. The old kinship clan certainly grew together for mutual protection and help of a band of equals; as that degenerated into a mere privileged caste of nobles, and became worse than useless for its original purpose, men formed other associations that had no bond of kindred, but a bond of mutual interest amidst the disorder of a rough period of transition. And once more we come across the guilds in quite early days of the new European society, and it is remarkable how much the purposes of these early guilds answer to those of the primitive kindred clan. To a great extent they were what we should now call benefit societies: they engaged to redeem their members from captivity; to set them up in business again if they were ruined; to pay their fines if they came into the clutch of the law. They were also clubs for good fellowship, and also (which again makes their analogy to the old clans the closer) drew their members together by the bond of religion, providing the sacrificial feast while our fore-fathers were still heathen, and paying for masses for the souls of their members when Christianity had become the popular religion; and there are instances of the chief work being defence by the strong hand, as in the case of protection against the Norse pirates in the tenth century. In short, it may well be said that from the first the history of the guilds is the true history of the Middle Ages. And we will remember, too, that they were in their early days in direct opposition to the authority of the period, which saw in them, as it was well warranted in doing, a threat of rebellious progress against the robbery of the poor and industrious by the rich and idle. In the Middle Ages, apart from those old Roman guilds, which were of handicraftsmen, this was the first character which the guilds took; leagues of the individually powerless freemen against the accidents of oppression, legal and illegal, held together by a religious bond according to the custom of the times.

To these about the eleventh century were superadded another set of guilds, whose main object was the protection of trade, and which soon became powerful, and establishing themselves in the towns, drew together with the corporations, the freemen of the towns, and were fused with them. They shared in the degeneration of the municipal aristocracies, which reached its height in the beginning of the thirteenth century, and with them were attacked by the third and last set of guilds, whose office was the organization and protection of the handicrafts. These of course had been growing up with the growth of the towns, and the increasing capacity for production, and at the time I mention were organized pretty completely, and embraced, I think, the whole of the handicrafts.

The greater part of the thirteenth century was taken up by the struggle between these new and quite democratic guilds, which were entirely composed of workmen; that struggle was partly a peaceable one. The municipalities could not quite keep the guilds from all participation in the government of the towns; their officers gradually crept into the corporations, and they began to influence the administration; but this peaceful revolution was supplemented by very hard fighting, especially in the north of Germany. The upshot of this double struggle was the complete victory of the workmen over the municipal aristocracies, and by the end of the thirteenth century the craft guilds, who no doubt had been fostered all along by the increasing productivity of labour, had the towns entirely in their power; but, although the municipal aristocracy had lost its privileged official position, the old families had not lost all their influence, and still formed a kind of middle-class nobility; this is exemplified clearly enough by the incidents in the struggle between the great town of Ghent and its feudal superior, the Earl of Flanders, in which men like James Van Artavelde and his sons clearly had a position akin to that of powerful rich men at the present day. The old struggle also was not forgotten; throughout the men of the mean crafts are on the revolutionary side; while the great crafts, led by the mariners, *i.e.*, the shippers, merchants, and so on, are loyalists.

This victory of the handicraftsmen brings us to the apex of the Middle Ages. Let us therefore stop a little to contrast the condition of labour at that period with its condition under the height of the classical period, and see what it has gained. The classical period gives us a class of privileged persons actually idle as far as any good purpose goes, supporting a huge class of parasites, and an enormous pauper population fed on *charity*, and all this founded on the labour of mere chattel slaves, who were fed, clothed and housed according to the convenience of their owners, just as beasts of burden were, but whom they had to buy with hard cash just as they had their horses and mules. There was a certain amount of labour done by freemen, or non-slaves rather, but that did not come to much, and I think we may class these few freemen among the parasites of the rich. The government of all this was aristocratic at first (tempered by the money-bag aristocracy), and at last mere absolutism founded on tax-gathering.

In the fully developed Middle Ages, on the other hand, we have a privileged class of land-holders deduced from the freemen of the conquering tribe, absolutely idle, supported by their serfs, who for their part are somewhat speedily turning into tenants, and so laying part of the foundations of the later middle-class. Between these two classes, which in the beginning of the Middle Ages were the essential constituents of society, lies the great body of the craftsmen, now gathered into towns administered by themselves, oppressed always, no doubt, legally by taxes, and often illegally by war on the part of the nobles, but free in their work except for such regulations as they have imposed on themselves, and the object of which in the main was the equitable distribution of employment, and the reward of employment throughout their whole body. Capitalism does not exist at this time; there is no great all-embracing world-market; production is for the supply of the neighbourhood, and only the surplus of it ever goes a dozen miles from the door of the worker. It must be added that every freeman has the use of land to support himself on, so that he does not depend on the caprice of the market for his bare necessities, and whether employer or employed, he neither sells himself, nor buys others, in the labour market under the rule of competition, but exchanges labour for labour directly with his neighbour, man to man and hand to hand.

Now, you will probably agree with me in thinking that this was a much better state of things for the worker than his condition under what have been called the "*free* peoples of antiquity," but whose freedom was confined to the rich and powerful. One other thing I note in this contrast, that whereas in the ancient world, the intelligence, the high mental qualities, which have made the ancient days so famous, came from the idle classes, who were in good sooth an aristocracy of intellect as well as of position, in the Middle Ages, the intelligence lay with the great craftsmen class,—and that again, I think, was a decided advantage, both for them and for us; since it has given us, amongst other treasures not so famous, but scarcely less glorious, the poems of Shakespeare.

Now, on this high tide of mediæval life supervened two things: the Black Death, and the gradual decay of the guilds, both of which got the times ready for the next great change in the condition of labour. I will say little about the first, space not serving for it. I will only remark first, that the Statute of Labourers of Edward III., which was one consequence of it, and which has been so useful to enquirers into the condition of labour at that time, represents in the account of wages and labour-hours to be drawn from it, the state of things *before* the terrible plague, not *after* it, since it was avowedly enacted against the labourers in order to lower their wages to the standard of reward before the Black Death.

Furthermore, I must say that all antiquarians must be fully conscious of the decline in art that took place in Northern Europe, and in England especially, after the reign of Edward III. Before the middle of the fourteenth century the English were in these matters abreast with, and in some matters ahead of, the Italians, and in the art of architecture especially, produced works which have never been surpassed, and seldom equalled. By the end of the fifteenth century our arts had for the most part become rude, unfinished and barbarous, and lacking altogether in that self-respect and confidence which the arts are always full of in their fine periods.

Looking carefully at the gradual change, I conclude that the Black Death was answerable for some of this degradation, but that the main part of it was the natural consequence of the great change which was coming over society. For during the next century, a new plague invaded Europe, compared with which the slaughter of the Black Death was but a trifle. That plague was the pest of Commercialism; capitalism aided by bureaucracy and nationalism, began to show itself, and took away from labour the hope of a happy life on the earth.

At the end of the fourteenth century, there were no journey-men in the guilds; every worker in them was certain to become a master if he only did his duty fairly; and the master was not the master in our sense of the word, he was the man who had learned his craft thoroughly, and could teach the apprentices their business, and all sorts of restrictions were laid on him to prevent him becoming a capitalist, *i.e.*, forcing men as good as himself to pay him for his privilege of providing them with work. But in the early days of the fifteenth century the journeyman began to appear; there were men in the workshops who were known as "servants," and, who though necessarily affiliated to the guild, and working under its regulations, would never become crafts-masters. They were few and unimportant enough, but they grew in numbers, till, *e.g.*, about 1480 the non-guildsmen of the merchant-tailors in London attempted to form a guild under the old craft guild, just as those latter had formed their guilds under the trades guilds. In this attempt they failed, showing thereby how the times were changing, and how employment for profit was raising its hideous head. This falling of the crafts guilds from their old simplicity of equality, was doubtless a token rather than a cause of the change. Capitalism was advancing from other

directions. The productivity of labour was increasing, though
slowly; more wealth was being produced, and men's greedy
desires grew with it. The landed nobility began to see how they
might recover their losses in war, and become as rich in relation
to other people as they had been when the latter were so poor;
and they were no longer contented, as they once were obliged to
be, to live on the rents of their land, whether those rents were
the enforced service of serfs, or the money rent of tenants, both
limited by the custom of the manor. The Peasants Rebellion in
England had foiled them in their attempt to rack-rent their
tenants, growing prosperous, by forcing them to pay serfs'
services on villeinage tenures as well as tenant's rent. But no
matter; in spite of the high wages and comfort of the craftsmen
and yeomen, *they* were the powerful people, since they were the
makers and interpreters of the laws, and since the meetings
round the Shire Oak and the folkmotes of the freemen of the
Hundred, and other such direct local assemblies, had been
swallowed up in the representative assembly, the central parliament, the King's taxing machine. So they set to work to steal, not
a purse here, or a bale of goods there, or the tolls of a market in
another place; but the very life and soul of the community, the
land of the country, which was of the more importance, as in
those days no direct rent could be got out of anything save the
land. They got the yeomen and tenants off the land by one
means or another; legal quibbling, direct cheating, down-right
violence; and so got hold of the lands and used their produce, not
for the livelihood of themselves and their retainers, but for profit.
The land of England, such of it as was used for cultivation, had
been mostly tillage where tillage was profitable; it was the
business of the land thieves to turn this tillage into pasture for
the sake of the sheep, *i.e.*, the wool for exportation. This game
not only drove the yeoman and tenant off the land, but the
labourer also, since, as More says "Many sheep and one shepherd
now take the place of many families." As a result, not only was a

pauper population created, but the towns were flooded by
crowds of the new free labourers, whom the guilds, grown
corrupt, were ready to receive as journeymen. The huckstering
landlord and the capitalist farmer drove the workman into the
hands of the new manufacturing capitalist, and a middle-class of
employers of labour was created, the chief business of whose
fathers was to resist the rich, and the business of whose sons was
to oppress the poor.

Thus fell the Society of the Middle Ages, by Capitalism establishing itself on the ruins of Feudality, and the rise of a middle-
class who were either parasites of the nobility, themselves
become commercial, trading on the grossest monopolies, and
exacting rack-rent, and practically doing the state no service—
partly parasites of the nobility, or partly employers living on the
profit wrung out of workmen employed at a very low rate of
wages. I have been giving the story of the change as it happened
in England. On the Continent the divorce of the people from the
land was not so sudden or complete, I think because there was
less resistance possible to the centralised bureaucracy here than
on the Continent. There, on the other hand, the rise of definite
nations with stiff political demarcations gave rise to most horrible
wars, which reduced the peasants to the last stage of misery,
hampered new-born commerce, and in the long run ruined the
land-owning aristocracy, and at last made the French Revolution
both possible and necessary. It is no exaggeration to say that
Germany is only now within the last twenty years recovering
from the Thirty Year's War which went on at the end of the
sixteenth and beginning of the seventeenth centuries.

But with the birth of capitalism and the world-market, the
relative importance of agriculture and manufacture began to
alter; and that again especially in England, a country so rich in
coal and minerals, and so well furnished with harbours on all
sides. The new-born power of making profit out of the employment of handicraftsmen had to be exercised and developed. The

craftsmen were in a changed position; they had been completely masters of their own work with other resources, which forbade the work mastering them; they were so no longer; they were working for other people, driven by competition to sell themselves at a poor price in the market. In short, they had become wage-slaves; but they were still handicraftsmen working in an isolated way. They were not being made the most of, and could only by the instruments of a timid scanty commerce. If they could have remained thus I think that they would have been less degraded then they became afterwards, and are now; but then the last word of progress would have been said, the hope of revolution would never have arisen.

What happened was very different. Capitalism was no sooner born than she was forced to sow the seed of her decay and final destruction; she was forced to develope the power of Labour to the utmost; that was indeed her work. The mechanical invention of man had lain dormant since the early days that had invented the plough, the cart, the row-boat, and the simple machines that help man's labour and do not supersede it, such as the grist-mill, the potter's wheel, the lathe, the simple loom, the crane, etc.; that invention was now to wake up, but not very suddenly; the fuller organisation of handicraft was to precede its abolition. I say when Capitalism began to grow towards manhood at the end of the sixteenth century, production was wholly by handicraft little organised.

The work of the seventeenth century was that gradual organisation by means of the division of labour. In handicraft (supposing a man to take no pleasure in his work, to be no artist) the single worker's whole intelligence is wasted on a piece of commonplace goods; a small part of that intelligence will suffice, if the whole of some one else's intelligence is employed in organising. Therefore, set him, the single man, at doing one small portion of that work, and you can soon dispense with almost all his intelligence, while at the same time you will quicken the habit of his hand, his mechanical power, prodigiously; in short, you will at last make of him a very delicate machine, or part of a machine, for performing the small piece of work you apportion to him; but you must take care that the whole machine of him and his fellows must be properly built up. This was the work of the seventeenth century. In the eighteenth it was complete, and the unit of labour was no longer a single man but a group of men.

Commerce was now, one would think, as well provided as she needed to be; but happily she could not stop there, or there would still have been no revolution possible for us. Now, indeed, she stirred up the sleeping invention of man, and with the latter half of the eighteenth century began that marvellous series of inventions, which one would have thought should have set mankind free from the greater part of his labour, but which, as it is, has done, on the face of it, little more than make a new and enormously rich middle-class, and multiply the working population many times over in order to provide them with due wage-slaves, who work not less, but more than they did in the days before the organisation of labour, and get not higher wages, but lower for their more burdensome labour.

My briefly told tale is over now, for I need not go through the often-told story of the fly-shuttle, the spinning jenny, the steam-engine, the power-loom, and the rest of it. I will only remark that the last development of machinery is to make the factory itself the machine, of which these wonderful machines, and the men that manage them (the most wonderful of all) are only parts. There remains only on this side of human life, production to wit, one thing to do as long as machine production lasts (which I prophecy will not be for ever). That one thing is this: The machines were invented that some men might work harder and others softer than they used to do, and they have well fulfilled their purpose; but though they have in that process seized hold of the bodies of the hard-working ones, the wage-slaves, though the factory has their bodies in its grip, it has not got hold of their intelligence, and does not want it, nay, sedulously keeps it out. Suppose that intelligence to wake up and to say, The hard work and the soft work, let us no longer keep these two separate for two classes of men, but throw them together and divide them equally amongst all, so that there should be no classes! In that case would not life in general, the only holy and sacred thing we know, be purified and made far holier by taking away from it the sorrow and misery that come of anxious seeking for toil, and the need for accepting the sickening burden. Surely that is so. Surely there is nothing in the machines themselves and the invention of man which created them, that they should forbid the true use of them, the lightening the burden of human labour.

That is what we Socialists under the machine and factory system are striving for at present, leaving the consideration of what is to be done to the machines and factories to future ages, who will be free to consider it, as we are not. Freedom first at any price, and then if possible happiness, which to my mind would be the certain result of freedom. Or are we free? I have told you what the condition of the civilised world in the days of the late Roman Republic, and the Absolutist Empire which followed it. What is its condition now that we have gone through chattel-slavery and serfdom to wage-slavery? It can be told in nearly the same words.

A privileged class partly composed of a landed nobility, partly of a money-bag aristocracy; a parasite class, ministering to their pleasures and their corruption, drinking of their cup, eating of their dish, flattering them and flattered by them but despised by them, and (woes me!) sharing in their crime of living on the misery of the poor. And those by whose labour they live? A huge population of miserable and hopeless labourers, to whom are superadded a crowd of paupers, far less joyous than the old Roman ones, fed by the fears, the remorse—the charity we call it—of the rich; and a few, a very few, free workmen, who as they work not for the workers, but the idle, must be turned back again to herd with the crowd of parasites aforesaid. Who can dare to say that this is not true of our society? And how does it differ from that of Roman corruption? Can its end be otherwise then—or worse?

Remember this, that in the days of that Roman corruption there was valiancy outside it which was ready to help the then world by destruction and new life combined; its enemies were the friends of the world, and were as good in their way as the early classical peoples had been in theirs, and I say they were outside that society, but at hand for its regeneration. All that the last two thousand years have used up; there is nothing outside civilisation that we can turn to for new birth; whatever there is to help us must come from within.

How are we to get at that? you will say. The answer to that question is the fact that we admit that the workers of to-day are wage-slaves. Those that feel themselves slaves must have been driven to desire freedom. But, again, what is the freedom which we desire? For the word has been used so often that men have forgotten its meaning. I think the answer is the freedom to develope our capacities to the utmost without injuring our neighbours. And how can that be done? By each of us working for the welfare of the whole of which we each form a part, and feeling sure that only so can we each of us fare well. Shall we not then have to give up a great deal in order to reach this point? Yes, we who are trying to bring people to that point will have to, but when people have reached it, they, when Socialism is realised, will turn round and find that their loss has only been imaginary. The rich man will have lost riches, *i.e.*, dominion over others, and find that he is happy; the intellectual man will have given up his claim to be worshipped by the masses, and will find that he is understood by them and loved by them—and the poor man, what has he to give up? He will have to give up his chance of becoming rich—a valuable possession truly—and he will find that he is not rich, but wealthy; that is, that he has whatever a man healthy in mind and body can wish for, and that poverty has become an evil dream but half remembered.

In short, even now, while the realisation of Socialism, though it is already going on, is neither desired nor understood by most men, the mere breath and rumour of its coming can at least hold out to true men who will join our ranks one gift at least—that they shall be glad to live and not afraid to die. And is that not a wonderful contrast to the spirit of the life of those who are still living placidly, because ignorantly, amidst the dishonesty of our present society? wherein how many there are, and those not always the poorest or most ignorant, but men of culture, men of genius, who do at once hate life and fear death. Friends, join us in helping to throw off this bugbear, so that you may be no longer wage-slaves or their masters, or their masters' parasites. So shall we be our own Goths, and at whatever cost break up again the new tyrannous Empire of Capitalism.

ARTICLES

THE LORD MAYOR'S SHOW

1884

I t would be a hard-hearted person indeed who could either
object seriously to or look sourly upon the Lord Mayor's
Show as a holiday pageant, an afternoon brightening-up of
the hideous and sordid streets of the "Great Wen," as Cobbett
called it; and considering the depths of the degradation of all
spectacular art at the present day, it would be too cruel to criticise
the spectacle of last Monday from an artistic point of view, even
if the columns of JUSTICE were the best place in which to do
so. But since the Fathers of the City have thought good in one
part of their show to call attention to an episode of London
history, the murder of Wat Tyler, it may be worth while for the
sake of the practical moral to recall to our readers the story of
which that murder was the climax; all the more as it has become
a sort of nursery tale in which the figures of the wise and pious
kingly youth, the sturdy loyal citizen, and the ruffianly agitator
have been made to stand out against a dark background of foolish
and ignorant armed peasants, knowing not what they asked for.

We will take our tale from that marvellous gallery of pictures
of the past, which a contemporary, the aristocratic priest, John
Froissart, wrought for us. Priest and Queen's Chaplain though
he was, his Gothic love of incident prevents his prejudice from
damaging his account of facts too much. Besides it seemed to
him so natural that such things should be, that he never thinks of

softening any enormity of the lordly tyranny which he served: *hypocritical* tyranny was the invention of a later age.

Says he:– ... "I will speak thereof as it was done, as I was informed, and of the incidents thereof. There was an usage in England and yet it is in diverse countries, that the noble men hath great franches over the Commons, and keepeth them in servage: that is their tenants ought by custom to labour the lords' lands, to gather and bring home their cornes, and some to thresh and to fanne, and by servage to make their hay, and hew their wood and bring it home: ... and there be more of these people in England than in any other realm.... These unhappy people began to stir saying, why should they be kept so under like beasts; the which they said they would no longer suffer, for they would be all one."

In short they objected to exploitation by means of serfdom. The worthy cannon then tells us of the "imagination of a foolish priest in the county of Kent, called John Ball," who on Sundays after mass used—in fact to hold open air meetings. Into his mouth Froissart puts simple and noble words by no means out of date at present, beginning thus; "Ah ye good people, the matter goeth not well to pass in England, nor shall do till every thing be common, and there be no villains nor gentlemen, but that we all be united together." John Ball was imprisoned by the Archbishop, but soon came out again by no means cured of his "imagination." The men of the home counties rose, saying that they would march on London, where they hoped to be well received, "and would so do to the King that there should not be one bondman left in England." They were 60,000 strong led by John Ball, Jack Straw and Wat Tyler, "who," says Froissart, "was indeed a tiler of houses, an ungracious person." The King's mother the Princess passing through their bands as she came from Canterbury received no sort of harm from them: the townsmen of Rochester were, says Froissart, "of the same secte" and received them well; they forced the captain of the Castle and

some other men-at-arms to go with them as their leaders, and
sent from Blackheath where they were encamped, Sir John
Newton the Captain of Rochester to lay their grievances before
the King; the result of which was that the King held a parley with
the leaders from his barge off Rotherhithe, but nothing came of
it; so they marched into London where they met with no resistance from the citizens; 30,000 of whom, says Froissart "were of
their own sect." There they broke open the Marshalsea Prison
and pillaged the Savoy, the palace of the Duke of Lancaster, the
King's uncle, who was as unpopular as need be: otherwise they
did little damage, considering how rough the times were.

The Mayor, Sir William Walworth was ready to attack them,
but the King and his court were panic-stricken and found the
good old plan of temporising and lying the most convenient. The
Earl of Salisbury and the wise men about the King said; "Sir, if
ye can appease them with fairness it were best, and to grant them
everything that they desire."

So a proclamation was issued that they should all draw
together to a fair plain place called Mile-End, whereas the people
of the city did sport them in the summer season. There the King
and his lords met them and asked what were their grievances,
"And such as understood him said, 'We wish that ye make us free
for ever, and that we may be no more bond, nor so reputed.'
'Sirs,' said the King, 'I am well agreed thereto; withdraw you
home to your own houses, and leave behind you of every village
two or three; and I shall cause writings to be made and seal them
with my seal, the which they shall have with them, containing
everything that ye demand; and to the intent that ye may be the
better assured I shall cause my banners to be delivered into every
bailswick, shire and county."

These promises broke the neck of the rebellion; the country
people took their papers and banners and went home happy we
must suppose with those very immaterial guarantees. But their
leaders knew their masters better and dared to try to hold matters

together still; and the next day (Saturday) the rebels met together on Smithfield some 20,000 strong, thither also came the King and his lords from Westminster, intending, as Froissart says, to leave London, but halting at St. Bartholomew's Church on sight of the rebels. Wat Tyler, seeing the hall, spurred up to the King; Froissart with mediæval minuteness gives a strange dramatic dialogue between the two; which was ended by the coming up of the Mayor with a small following secretly armed. It was then pretty much a word and a blow, Walworth unhorsed Wat with a sword stroke to the head, and one Standish or Cavendish, a squire of the King's, finished him with his sword as he lay on the ground. The angry people, seeing their leader fall, advanced with bent bows, but the King met them again boldly enough, promised all redress, and offered himself their captain; and the rebels uncertain and leaderless again began to disperse. Meanwhile the 'party of order' had been drawing to a head, and a large body of well-armed men, seven or eight thousand, came on the field. The King, says the chronicler, prevented a general onslaught of the knights and men-at-arms on the now broken people, but their leaders and spokesmen were forced to deliver up the banners and letters of redress they had received, which latter were torn up before their eyes, and the whole host was dispersed.

John Ball and Jack Straw were hunted out and slain, and their heads with Wat Tyler's stuck on London Bridge.

Then came the reaction of which Froissart tells with great naiveté. The king made a progress through Kent, at every town and village the ring-leaders were hunted out and dealt with; the letters promising redress were torn up solemnly before the people, and the great peril for the privileged was got over. Froissart leaves no doubt in our minds as to how that peril struck him; for he connects this rising of the Kentishmen with the Revolt of Ghent, and the rising of the 'unhappy people with the iron mallets at Paris.' But all these things were but as the stirring among the dry bones, terrible as they semed (*sic*) to the rich of that period, and it took a long course of economic events before the power of privilege was even shaken.

Meantime we need make no mistake about the cause for which Wat Tyler and his worthier associate John Ball fell; they were fighting against the fleecing of the people by that particular form of fleecing then in fashion, viz.: serfdom or villeinage, which was already beginning to wane before the advance of the industrial gilds. We need not grumble therefore if the sword of St. Paul in the city arms is sometimes innocently taken for Wat Tyler's instrument of martyrdom, however little the worthy city fathers may like the construction we should put on that legend. Nor will we say that he and John Ball died for nothing, however doleful is the story (an oft repeated one) of the stout men of Kent breaking up half in fear and irresolution, half deluded by the lies and empty promises of their masters, to whom, as ever, any course seemed good that enabled them to keep the people down.

WHY WE CELEBRATE
THE COMMUNE OF PARIS

1887

The "moons and the days" have brought us round again to the anniversary of the greatest tragedy of modern times, the Commune of Paris of 1871, and with it the recurring duty for all Socialists of celebrating it both enthusiastically and intelligently. By this time the blatant slanders with which the temporarily unsuccessful cause was assailed when the event was yet fresh in men's minds have sunk into the dull gulf of lies, hypocritical concealments, and false deductions, which is called bourgeois history, or have become a dim but deeply rooted superstition in the minds of those who have information enough to have heard of the Commune, and ignorance enough to accept the bourgeois legend of it as history.

Once more it is our duty to raise the whole story out of this poisonous gloom and bring it to the light of day, so that on the one hand those who are not yet touched by Socialism may learn that there was a principle which animated those who defended revolutionary Paris against the mingled dregs of the woeful period of the Second Empire, and that that principle is still alive to-day in the hearts of many thousands of workers throughout civilisation, and year by year and day by day is growing in strength and in the hold it has of the disinherited masses of our false society; and on the other hand that we Socialists may

soberly note what went on in this story, and may take both
warning and encouragement from its events. I have heard it said,
and by good Socialists too, that it is a mistake to commemorate a
defeat; but it seems to me that this means looking not at this
event only, but at all history in too narrow a way. The Commune
of Paris is but one link in the struggle which has gone on through
all history of the oppressed against the oppressors; and without
all the defeats of past times we should now have no hope of the
final victory. Neither are we yet sufficiently removed in time
from the events to judge how far it was even possible to avoid the
open conflict at the time, or to appreciate the question as to what
would have become of the revolutionary cause if Paris had
tamely yielded itself up to the perfidy of Thiers and his allies.
One thing, on the other hand, we are sure of, that this great
tragedy has definitely and irrevocably elevated the cause of
Socialism to all those who are prepared to look on the cause
seriously, and refuse to admit the possibility of ultimate defeat.
For I say solemnly and deliberately that if it happens to those of
us now living to take part in such another tragedy it will be rather
well for them than ill for them. Truly it is harder to live for a
cause than to die for it, and it injures a man's dignity and self-
respect to be always making noisy professions of devotion to a
cause before the field is stricken, on which he is to fight in the
body. But with the chance of bodily sacrifice close a-head there
come also times of trial which either raise a man to the due tragic
pitch or cast him aside as a useless and empty vapourer. To use a
transparent metaphor, on the march to the field of battle there
are plenty of opportunities for the faint-hearted to fall out of the
ranks, and many will do so whose courage and devotion were
neither doubted by others nor by themselves while the day of
actual battle was far distant. So such times of trial are good
because they are times of trial; and we may well think that few
indeed of those who fell sixteen years ago, who exposed
themselves to death and wounds at all adventure, were mere

accidental braggarts caught in the trap. Of those whose names are well known this was far from being the case, and who can doubt that the nameless multitude who died so heroically had sacrificed day by day other things than life, before it came to that?

Furthermore, it must surely be rather more than doubtful to all thoughtful men if the mere exercise of every-day and civil virtues, even when directed towards the social end, will suffice to draw the world out of its present misery and confusion. Consider the enormous mass of people so degraded by their circumstances that they can scarcely understand any hope for their redemption that can be put before them in peaceful and constitutional times. Yet these are the very people for whom we are working; and are they to have no hand in the work, then? is it to be once more according to the degrading Positivist motto, "everything *for* you, nothing *by* you?" Meanwhile in these people, unless we Socialists are all wrong, there are seeds of manly and social feeling, capable of large development; and surely when the time comes that their hope will be made manifest, as it was in the time of the Commune, and will lie before them for their hands to take, they will then have part in the work indeed, and by the act of doing so will at once raise themselves out of the slough of degradation into which our false society has cast them and in which it keeps them. The revolution itself will raise those for whom the revolution must be made. The newborn hope translated into action will develop their human and social qualities, and the struggle itself will fit them to receive the benefits of the new life which revolution will make possible for them. It is for boldly seizing the opportunity offered for thus elevating the mass of the workers into heroism that we now celebrate the men of the Commune of Paris. True they failed in conquering immediate material freedom for the people, but they quickened and strengthened the ideas of freedom by their courageous action and made our hope of to-day possible; and if to-day any one doubts that they were fighting for the emancipation of labour, their enemies at the time had no doubt about the matter. They saw in them no mere political opponents, but "enemies of society," people who could not live in the same world with them, because the basis of their ideas of life was different—to wit, humanity, not property. This was why the fall of the Commune was celebrated by such hecatombs sacrificed to the bourgeois god, Mammon; by such a riot of blood and cruelty on the part of the conquerors as quite literally has no parallel in modern times. And it is by that same token that we honour them as the foundation-stone of the new world that is to be.

REVOLUTIONARY CALENDAR: WAT TYLER

1888

Wat Tyler.—Wat Tyler, *i.e.*, Walter, the tiler or thatcher, was an artisan of Dartford, in Kent, and became a leader in the great peasant rebellion which took place in England in the early years of Richard II (1381), and which was much more dangerous to the tyranny of the day than is usually supposed; it spread from the north of East Anglia, all through Essex and Kent, and along the south coast to Exeter. The immediate occasion of Wat Tyler's own rebellion as related by the chroniclers, was his resistance to a bailiff, who, calling for the poll-tax then being levied by the very unpopular Government, treated his young daughter brutally, and was slain by Wat with his lath-rending axe. The rebellion, however, in which the valiant tiler was a leader, had much deeper roots than resistance to a mere tax. It was a protest against the reaction of the landlords against the inevitable movement which was abolishing serfdom; the serfs were gradually turning into tenants, and much unfree *land* was being held by free *men*; and these the landlords were attempting to force into serfdom on the ground that their lands were the lands of serfs, and that therefore they must be serfs. Wat Tyler and the Kentish bands gathered at Blackheath on June 11, 1381, and on the next day marched thence into London, where the feeling of the people was with them and where they met with no resistance. The Court was terrified by a visit they paid to the Tower, and the King prepared to leave London; on his way occurred the celebrated scene in Smithfield, where Wat Tyler was basely assassinated while pleading the People's Cause under safe conduct. The King promised the enraged people whatever they demanded, and thus broke up their gathering, and as a matter of course kept his promise afterwards by wholesale murders amongst his helpless and scattered people. Nevertheless, though the rebellion was put down it had slain the reaction it was aimed at before it died itself, and the extinction of serfdom in England went on faster and faster.

SOCIALISM FROM THE ROOT UP

1886

Chapter I

ANCIENT SOCIETY

In beginning this series on Socialism, we think it necessary to prelude the matter which may appear to interest more immediately us now living, by a brief allusion to the history of the past.

Our adversaries are sometimes forward to remind us that the present system with which we are so discontented, has been made by the growth of ages, and that our wills are impotent to change it; they do not see that in stating this fact they are condemning their own position. Our business is to recognise the coming change, to clear away obstacles to it, to accept it, and to be ready to organise it in detail. Our opponents, on the contrary, are trying consciously to stay that very evolution at the point which it has reached to-day; they are attempting to turn the transient into the eternal; therefore, for them history has no lessons, while to us it gives both encouragement and warning which we cannot afford to disregard. The hopes for the industrialism of the future are involved in its struggles in the past; which, indeed, since they have built up the present system, and placed us amidst its struggle towards change, have really forced us whether we will it or not, to help forward that change.

The modern civilised State has been developed by the antagonism between individual and social interests, which has transformed primitive Society into Civilisation. The conditions of mere savage life recognised nothing but the satisfaction of the immediate needs of the individual; this condition of complete want of co-operation yielded to primitive Communism as the powers of man grew, and he began to perceive that he could do more than satisfy his daily needs for food and shelter. By this time he had found that he could aid nature in forcing the earth to produce livelihood for him; the hill and forest became something more to him than the place where berries and roots grew, and wild creatures lived, the land became pasture ground to him, and at last amid some races ground for tillage.

But the wealth of man still grew, and change came with its growth; the land was common in the sense that it was not the property of individuals, but it was not common to all comers; primitive society was formed, and man was no longer a mass of individuals, but the groups of this primitive society were narrow and exclusive; the unit of Society was the *Gens*, a group of blood-relations at peace among themselves, but which group was hostile to all other groups; within the Gens wealth was common to all its members, without it wealth was prize of war.

This condition of war necessarily developed leadership amongst men; successful warriors gained predominance over the other members of the Gens, and since the increasing powers of production afforded more wealth to be disposed of above the mere necessities of each man, these warrior leaders began to get to themselves larger shares of the wealth than others, and so the primitive communism of wealth began to be transformed into individual ownership.

The Tribe now took the place of the Gens; this was a larger and more artificial group, in which blood relationship was conventionally assumed. In it, however, there was by no means mere individual ownership, although, as said above, Communism had been broken into; the tribe at large disposed of the use of the land according to certain arbitrary arrangements, but did not admit ownership in it to individuals. Under the tribal system also slavery was developed, so that class Society had fairly began (*sic*).

The Tribe in its turn melted into a larger and still more artificial body, the People—a congeries of many tribes, the ancient
Gothic-Teutonic name for which—*theoth*—is still preserved in
such names as *Theo*bald. This was the last development of Barbarism; nor was there much change in the conditions of wealth
under it from those obtaining among the Tribe, although it held
in it something more than the mere *germs* of feudalism.

Finally, ancient Barbarism was transformed into ancient
Civilisation, which, as the name implies, took the form of the life
of the city. With these cities political life began, together with the
systematization of the old beliefs into a regular worship. The
religion of Barbarism was the worship of the ancestors of the
tribe, mingled with fetichism (*sic*), which was the first universal
religion, and may best be described as a state of mind in which
the universe was conceived of as a system of animated beings to
be feared and propitiated by man. This was transformed into
what may be called city patriotism, which summed up the whole
religion of the city, and which was the real religion of the Greeks
and Romans in their progressive period, and of all the then
progressive races of mankind, including the Hebrew. In these
cities slavery speedily developed until it embraced nearly the
whole of industrialism, the main business of the free citizens
being the aggrandizement of their city by war.[1] For the cities
were as hostile to each other as the tribes had been.

The course of events towards further transformation was that
in the East the cities formed federations which gradually fell
under the domination of bureaucratic and absolute monarchies,
of which China still remains as an example. The Greek and Latin
cities carried on the progress of human intelligence, but did not
escape corruption and transformation.

Amongst the Greeks the individual struggle for pre-eminence
gradually broke down the city patriotism, and led the way

towards the domination of mere military and political intrigue and confusion, till the independence of Greece was finally trampled out by the power of Rome, now corrupted also. For during this time in Rome the struggle of the plebeian order—or inferior tribes of which the city was composed—with the conservative oligarchy—that is, the three most ancient and consequently leading tribes—had developed a middle-class living on the profits derived from slave labour, which broke up the old city republic and led to the formation of a commercial and tax-gathering empire, founded on slavery, whose subjects were devoid of all political rights, and in which the triumph of individualism was complete. Indeed, this same struggle had taken place in one way or another in the Greek cities also. Thus was all public spirit extinguished. The natural greed of commercialism gradually ate up the wealth of the empire: even slave labour became unprofitable. The landlords were ruined; the taxes could not be paid; and meanwhile the Roman soldier, once a citizen religiously devoted to his city, became a bribed hireling, till at last no bribe was high enough to induce a civilised man to fight, and the Roman legions were manned by the very barbarians whose kinsmen were attacking the empire from without.

Thus was ancient civilization delivered over to the Barbarians, fresh from their tribal communism, and once more the antagonism of individual and common rights was exemplified in the two streams of Barbarian and Roman ideas, from the union of which was formed the society of the next great epoch—the Middle Ages.

1   The Greeks added to this the practice of the higher arts and literature, neither of which the Romans possessed in their progressive period.

Chapter II

MEDIÆVAL SOCIETY

We have now to deal with that Mediæval Society which was based on the fusion of ideas of tribal communism and Roman individualism and bureaucracy. The fullest, and one may say the most pedantic type of this society is to be found in the Mediæval German Empire; it was modified somewhat in other countries; in France by the fact that several of the other potentates, as, *e.g.*, the Duke of Burgundy, were theoretically independent of the King, and practically were often at least as powerful. In England, on the contrary, the monarchy soon gained complete predominance over the great barons, and a kind of bureaucracy soon sprang up which interfered with the full working of the feudal system.

The theory of this feudal system is the existence of an unbroken chain of service from the serf up to the emperor, and of protection from the emperor down to the serf; it recognises no absolute ownership of land; God is the one owner of the earth, the emperor and his kings are his vice-gerents there, who may devolve their authority to their feudal vassals, and they in turn to theirs, and so on till it reaches the serf, the proletarian, on whom all this hierarchy lives, and who has no rights as regard his own lord except protection from others outside the manor that he lives and works on; to him his personal lord was the incarnation of the compulsion and protection of God, which all men acknowledged and looked for.

It is quite clear that this system was mixed up with religious ideas of some sort; accordingly, we find that the Middle Ages had a distinct religion of their own, developed from that early Christianity which was one of the forces that broke up the Roman Empire. As long as that Empire lasted in its integrity, Christianity was purely individualistic; it bade every man do his best for his future in another world, and had no commands to give about the government of this world except to obey "the powers that be" in non-religious matters, in order to escape troubles and complications which might distract his attention from the kingdom of God.

But in Mediæval Christianity, although this idea of individual devotion to the perfection of the next world still existed, it was kept in the background, and was almost dormant in the presence of the idea of the *Church*, which was not merely a link between the earthly and the heavenly kingdoms, but even may be said to have brought the kingdom of heaven to earth by breathing its spirit into the temporal power, which it recognised as another manifestation of its own authority. Therefore, the struggles of the Temporal and Spiritual Powers, which form so large a part of the history of the Middle Ages, were not the result of antagonism of ideas between the two, but came of the tendency of one side of the great organisation of Society to absorb the other without rejecting its theory; in short, on the one hand the Church was political and social rather than religious, while on the other the State was at least as much religious as it was political and social.

Such, then, was the theory of Mediæval Society; but apart from whatever of oppression on life and thought was inherent in it, the practice of the theory was liable to many abuses, to which the obvious confusion and misery of the times are mostly referable. These abuses again were met by a protest in the form of almost constant rebellion against Society, of which one may take as examples the organised vagabondage of Middle Europe, the Jacquerie in France, and in England what may be called the chronic rebellion of the Foresters, which produced such an impression on the minds of the people, that it has given birth to the ballad epic known by the name of its mythical hero, Robin Hood. Resistance to authority and contempt of the "Rights of Property" are the leading ideas in this rough but noble poetry.

Besides these irregular protests against the oppression of the epoch, there was another factor at work in its modification—the Gilds, which forced themselves into the system, and were accepted as a regular part of it.

The ideas which went with the survivals of the primitive communism of the tribes were, on the one hand, absorbed into the feudal system and formed part of it, but on the other, they developed associations for mutual protection and help, which at first were merely a kind of benefit societies according to the ideas of the times. These were followed by associations for the protection of trade, which were called the gilds-merchant. From these the development was two-fold: they were partly transformed into the corporations of the free towns, which had already began (*sic*) to be founded from other developments, and partly into the craft-gilds, or organisations for the protection and regulation of handicrafts—which latter were the result of a radical reform of the gilds-merchant, accomplished not without a severe struggle, often accompanied by actual and very bitter war. The last remains of these craft-gilds are traceable in the names of the city companies of London.

It should be noted that this tendency to association was bitterly opposed in its early days by the potentates of both Church and State, especially in those countries which had been more under the influence of the Roman empire. But in the long-run it could not be resisted, and at last both the gilds and the free towns which their emancipated labour had created or developed were favoured (as well as fleeced) by the bureaucratic kings as a make-weight to the powerful nobles and the Church.

The condition of one part of mediæval life industrial was thus quite altered. In the earlier Middle Ages the serf not only did all the field-work, but also most of the handicrafts, which now fell entirely into the hands of the gilds. It must be noted also that in their best days there were no mere journeymen in these crafts; a workshop was manned simply by the workman and his apprentices, who would, when their time was out, become members of the gild like himself: mastership, in our sense of the word, was unknown.

By about the year 1350 the craft-gilds were fully developed and triumphant; and that date may conveniently be accepted as the end of the first part of the Middle Ages.

By this time serfdom generally was beginning to yield to the change introduced by the gilds and free towns: the field serfs partly drifted into the towns and became affiliated to the gilds, and partly became free men, though living on lands whose tenure was unfree—copyholders, we should call them. This movement towards the break-up of serfdom is marked by the peasant's war in England led by Wat Tyler and John Ball in Kent, and John Litster (dyer) in East Anglia, which was the answer of the combined yeomen, emancipated and unemancipated serfs, to the attempt of the nobles to check the movement.

But the development of the craft-gilds and the flocking in of the freed serfs into the towns laid the foundations for another change in industrialism: with the second part of the mediæval period appears the journeyman, or so-called free labourer. Besides the craftsmaster and his apprentices, the workshop now had these "free labourers" in it—unprivileged workmen, that is, who were nevertheless under the domination of the gild, and compelled to affiliation with it. The gildsmen now began to be privileged workmen; and with them began the foundation of the present middle-class, whose development from this source went on to meet its other development on the side of trade which was now becoming noticeable. In 1453 Constantinople was taken by the Turks; the art of printing was spreading; Greek manuscripts were being discovered and read; a thirst for new or received learning, outside the superstitions of the mediæval Church and the quaint, curiously perverted and half-understood remains of popular traditions, was arising, and all was getting ready for the transformation of mediæval into modern or commercial society.

Chapter III

THE BREAK-UP OF FEUDALISM

The period of change from the feudal system into that of commerce is so important, and so significant to our subject, that it demands a separate chapter.

The beginning of the sixteenth century found, as we have said, the craft-gilds corrupted into privileged bodies holding within them two orders of workmen—the privileged and the unprivileged—the two forming the germ of a society founded on capital and wage-labour. The privileged workmen became middle-class; the unprivileged, proletarians.

But apart from the gilds, the two classes were being created by the development of commerce, which needed them both as instruments for her progress. Mediæval commerce knew nothing of capitalistic exchange; the demands of local markets were supplied by the direct exchange of the superfluity of the produce of the various districts and countries. All this was now being changed, and a world-market was being formed, into which all commodities had to pass; and a huckstering class grew up for the carrying on of this new commerce, and soon attained to power, amidst the rapid break-up of the old hierarchical society with its duly ordered grades.

The fall of Constantinople, which was followed in thirty years by the discovery of America, was a token of this great change.

The Mediterranean was no longer the great commercial sea, with nothing beyond it but a few outlying stations. The towns of Central Europe—*e.g.*, Augsburg, Nuremburg, Bruges, and the Hanse towns—were now sharing the market with Venice and Genoa, the children of Constantinople: there was no longer one great commanding city in Europe. But it was not only the rise in the commercial towns that was overturning feudal society. As they conquered their enemy, the feudal nobles, they fell into the clutches of bureaucratic monarchs, who either seized on them for their own possessions, or used them as tools for their projects on conquest and centralisation. Charles V., *e.g.*, played this game through South Germany, Austria, and the Netherlands, and with Venice, under cover of the so-called "Holy Roman Empire," while at the same time he had fallen into possession of Spain by marriage; and disregarding his sham feudal empire, he bent all his efforts into turning these countries into a real bureaucratic State. In France the last liberties of the towns were crushed out. In England the plunder of the religious houses enabled Henry VIII. to found a new nobility, subservient to his own absolutism, in place of the ancient feudal nobility destroyed by their late civil war.

Everywhere the modern political bureaucratic *nation* was being developed. In France the long and fierce wars of the Burgundian and Armagnac factions gave opportunity for the consolidation of the monarchy, which was at last effected by Louis XI., the forerunner of the most successful king of France and the last successful one—Louis XIV. In England the Wars of the Roses were not so bitter as the French wars, and the people took small part in them, except as vassals or the households of the contending nobles; but they nevertheless played their part in the disruption of feudality, not only by the thinning-out of the nobles slain in battle or on the scaffold, but also by helping directly to draw England into the world-market.

Under the mediæval system the workmen, protected and

oppressed by the lords of the manor and the gilds, were not available for the needs of commerce. The serfs ate up the part of the produce spared them by their lords; the gild craftsmen sold the produce of their own hands to their neighbours without the help of a middle-man. In neither case was there anything left over for the supply of a great market.

But England, one of the best pasture countries of the world, had in her even then capacities for profit-grinding, if the tillage system of the manor and the yeoman's holdings could be got rid of. The landowners, ruined by their long war, saw the demand for English wool, and set themselves to the task of helping evolution with much of the vigour and unscrupulous petti-fogging which has since won for their race the temporary command of the world-market. The tenants were rack-rented, the yeomen were expropriated, the labourers driven off the land into the towns, there to work as "free" labourers, and England thus contributed her share to commerce, paying for it with nothing more important than the loss of the rough joviality, plenty, and independence of spirit, which once attracted the admiration of foreigners more crushed by the feudal system and their abuses than the English were.

Thus all over Europe commercialism was rising. New needs were being discovered by men who were gaining fresh mastery over nature, and were set free from old restraints to struggle for individual pre-eminence. A fresh intelligence and mental energy was shedding its light over the more sordid side of the period of change. The study of the Greek literature at first hand was aiding this new intelligence among cultivated men, and also, since they did but half understand its spirit, was warping their minds into fresh error. Art was no longer religious and simple—the harmo-nious expression of the thought of the people—but was growing more and more ambitiously individualistic and arrogant, and at the same time grew more and more retrospective and tainted with pedantry.

Amidst all this it is clear that the old religion would no longer
serve the new spirit of the times. The Mediæval Church, the
kingdom of heaven on earth, in full sympathy with the temporal
hierarchy, in which also every one had his divinely appointed
place, and which restricted commerce and forbade usury, such a
Church was no religion for the new commercialism; its religion
must have nothing to do with the business of this world; so the
individualist ethics of Early Christianity, which had been kept in
the background during the period of the Mediæval Church, were
once more brought to the front and took the place of the corporate ethics of that Church, of which each one of the "faithful"
was but a part. Whatever base uses their enthusiasm was put to
by cooler heads, this revived Christianity took a real hold on
most of the progressive minds of the period, especially in the
north; so that Protestantism became the real religion of the
epoch, and even permeated Catholicism and gave it whatever
true vitality it had; for its political part was an unreal survival
from the Mediæval Church, and whatever of it was of any force
became the mere ally of bureaucracy; a word which applies to the
Protestant Churches just as much as the Catholic; and, in fact,
everywhere the new religion became the useful servant of
Commercialism, first by providing a new army of officials always
subservient to the authority of government, and secondly by
holding out to the people hopes outside their wretched life on
earth, so as to quiet their discontent by turning their earthly
aspirations heavenward. On the one hand like Early Christianity,
it bade let the world alone to compete for the possession of
privilege, and bade the poor pay no heed to the passing
oppression of the day, which could not deprive them of their true
reward in another world; but unlike Early Christianity, on the
other hand it shared in the possession of privilege, and actively
helped in the oppression which it counselled the oppressed not
to rebel against. But, as a truly distinct and equal power beside
the State, the Church was extinct; it was a mere salaried adjunct

of the State. The story, moreover, of the robbery by private persons of the public property which the Mediæval Church once held, was a disgraceful one everywhere, but nowhere so disgraceful as in England.

But while modern Europe was developing for itself a new economy, a new religion, and a new patriotism, the change did not take place without a protest of the disappointed hopes of the people in the form of fresh rebellion; though it was little heeded amidst the furious wars for the place and power of kings, and the establishment of political boundaries of the newly made "nations." The Peasant War in Germany, and the revolt of the Anabaptists, are, so to say, the funeral torches of the Middle Ages. The first was much of the nature of other mediæval insurrections, except that it was fiercer and longer lived; it ends the series of outbreaks which had been so common in England during the first years of the century. The revolt of the Anabaptists was an attempt to realise the kingdom of God upon earth literally and simply in a Communistic Society based on supernaturalism, and was a protest of ignorant and oppressed men against the hardening of Christianity into bourgeois Protestantism, and of the hardening of feudal oppression into commercial exploitation.

Thus, then, was the feudal system broken down, to give place to a new world, whose government, under cover of carrying on the old monarchies and varied classes of feudality, was employed in one business only, the consolidation and continuance of the absolute property of the individual. It is true that in carrying out this function, the new society used the forms of the old, and asserted hereditary rights stiffly enough; but this was only in its transition from the old to the new. In truth the spirit of the Middle Ages was dead, and its theory of society and authority in Church and State was gone. The kingdom of heaven of the Mediæval Church had left the earth, and did not concern itself with its doings except so far as they constituted theological holiness or sins. God no longer owned the land allowing human beings to use it after a divinely ordained scheme. It was now the *property* of the absolute monarch, who might give it to whomsoever he would; and it was only for a brief space that a dim shadow of feudal responsibility clung to the landowner.

Serfdom was gone, and the gilds were now but close corporations of privileged workmen, or of employers of labour. The ordinary workman was now "free." That is to say he could work where and how he pleased, *if* he could find some one who would set him to work at the price of taking from him a part of the produce of his labour; which labour was now a commodity to be bought and sold in the market as the body of the chattel-slave once had been.

Of the working of this new form of privilege and slavery we shall see more in our next chapter.

Chapter IV

MODERN SOCIETY:
EARLY STAGES

By the beginning of the seventeenth century the central-ising, bureaucratic monarchies were fairly established: nay, in France at least, they were even showing the birth of modern party-government, which since—carried on, indeed, under the veil of constitutionalism—has been the type of modern government. Richelieu—the Bismarck of his time and country—begins the series of prime ministers or real temporary kings, who govern in the interest of class society, not much encumbered and a good deal protected by their cloaks, the hered-itary formal sham kings. In England this prime-ministership was more incomplete, though men like Burleigh approached the type. Elizabeth reduced the Tudor monarchy to an absurdity, a very burlesque of monarchy, under which flourished rankly an utterly unprincipled and corrupt struggle for the satisfaction of individual ambition and greed. This grew still more rankly, perhaps, under James I., who added mere cowardice to all the other vices which are more common to arbitrary high place and power.

As to the condition of the people during the latter years of the sixteenth and beginning of the seventeenth century, the economical and religious revolution which had taken place had oppressed them terribly, and the "free workman" had to feel the full force of the causes which had presented him with his "freedom" in the interest of growing commerce. In England, on the one hand, the expropriation of the yeomanry from the land and the conversion of tillage into pasture had provided a large population of these free workmen, who, on the other hand, were not speedily worked up by the still scanty manufactures of the country, but made a sort of semi-vagabond population, troublesome enough to the upper and middle classes. The laws made against these paupers in the reigns of Henry VIII. and Edward VI. were absolutely ferocious, and men were hanged out of the way by the thousand.

But in the reign of Elizabeth it was found out that even this was not enough to cure the evil, which of course had been much aggravated by the suppression of the religious houses, part of whose function was the housing and feeding of any part of the workmen temporarily displaced. A Poor Law, therefore, was passed for dealing with this misery, and strange to say, it was far more humane than might have been expected from the way in which the poor had been dealt with up to that time; so much so, indeed, that the utilitarian *philanthropists* of the beginning of this century felt themselves obliged to deal with it in a very severe way, which left us a Poor Law as inhumane—or let us say as cruel—as could well be. Toward the middle of the seventeenth century things began to improve with our working population: the growth of the towns stimulated agriculture, and tillage began to revive again, though of course under the new system of cultivation for profit. Matters were in fact settling down, and preparing the country for a time of something like prosperity for the new revolution in industry.

The condition of the people was on the whole worse on the Continent than in England. Serfdom was by no means extinct in France and, especially, in Germany, and that serfdom was far more burdensome and searching side by side with the exploitation of the market than it had been in the feudal period. Other survivals of the mediæval epoch there were also—*e.g.*, in Germany the gilds had still some life and power, and the people were not utterly divorced from the land as in England, although the predominant competition of the markets prevented whatever good might linger in these half-extinct customs from being for the benefit of the people. At the same time the populations were crushed by the frightful wars which passed over them—in all which religion was the immediate excuse.

The first of this series was the war carried on in Holland against the Catholic foreigners—the Spaniards—into whose hands they had been thrown by the family affairs of Charles V. Although noblemen took up the side of the rebels—*e.g.*, Egmont and Horn, executed for so doing—this war was in the main a way of the bourgeois democracy on behalf of Protestantism, embittered by the feeling of a Teutonic race against a Latinised one. There is to be found in it even some foretaste of the revolutionary *sanscullote* element, as shown by the extreme bitterness of the ruder seafaring population, the men whose hats bore the inscription, "Better Turk than Pope."

In Germany the struggle known as the "Thirty Years' War" was between the great vassals of the German empire, the shadow of whose former power was used for the aggrandisement of the house of Charles V., and also for the enforcement of Catholicism on the more northern countries. It must be remembered, by the way, that these countries were to the full as absolutist as those which obeyed the bidding of the Emperor. This miserable war, after inflicting the most terrible suffering on the unhappy people, who were throughout treated with far less mercy and consideration than if they had been beasts; after having crushed the rising intelligence of Germany into a condition from which it has only arisen in days close to our own, dribbled out in a miserable and aimless manner, leaving the limits of Protestant and Catholic pretty much where it had found them: but it also left the people quite defenceless against their masters, the bureaucratic kings and knights.

In France this religious struggle took a very bitter form, but it was far more political than in Germany. The leaders were even prepared to change their creed when driven into a corner—as Henry of Navarre at the time of the Massacre of St. Bartholomew. In France the popular sympathy was by no means in favour of Protestantism: the Massacre of St. Bartholomew, which inflicted such a terrible blow on the Hugenot (*sic*) cause, would otherwise have been hardly possible. It is true that the great Hugenot (*sic*) leader, Henry of Navarre, became Hugenot (*sic*) king of France, but his accession did not carry with it a triumph as a consequence. Henry had to adjure Protestantism; a Protestant king of France was impossible.

The great struggle in England came later, and consequently probably the victory was more decided on the Puritan side. The enthusiasm with which Mary Tudor—"Bloody Mary"—was received, and the Catholic insurrections in the reign of her successor, showed that there was at first some popular feeling on the Catholic side; but by the time of James I. Catholicism was dead in England. The Book of Sports issued by his Government, which encouraged the people to play various games on Sunday, was widely received as an outrage on the feelings of the growing middle-class in town and country; and all was tending towards the irreconcilable quarrel which took place in the next reign between the Court and the Bourgeoisie, and which was nearly as much religious as political. For the rest, the Parliamentary party was on the advancing line of history both as regards politics and religion, and the King's party was simply reactionary; but the war was at furthest waged by a nobility inspired by a kind of romantic after-glow of mediæval chivalry. The successful outcome of the individual ambition of Cromwell extinguished whatever aspirations towards republicanism were cherished by a few purists, as well as the enthusiasm of the wild sectaries whose hopes of a rule of saints on the earth were tinged by some kind of communistic ideas; which were further fore-shadowed by the Levellers, though perverted by the mere asceticism which they held. Nevertheless, these men may be paralleled to the Anabaptists of Münster, although the latter were quite mediæval in spirit, and their fanatic religion had little in common with Puritanism; and though, also, the steady power of bourgeois rule concentrated in Cromwell's absolutism forbade them any opportunity of approaching even the most temporary realisation of their idea. Meanwhile England was unable to endure the weight of the absolute rule of Cromwell, lined with fully developed Puritanism, and a few plotters were allowed to restore the Stuart monarch, under whom the wild religion of the armed men—the victors over the nobility of England and their revived sham chivalry—sank into mere Quakerism, and the religious war was at [an] end, except for a few smouldering embers among the Cameronians in Scotland.

Meantime in France the last remnants of the old feudalism struggled in the party warfare of the "Fronde" against Mazarin and his bureaucracy of simple corruption, till Louis XIV. put the coping-stone on the French monarchy by forcing his nobility, high and low, into the position of his courtiers, while his minister Colbert developed the monarchy as a tax-gathering machine by the care and talent with which he fostered the manufactures of France, which just before his time were at a very low ebb; so that there was no need to touch the revenues of the nobility, who were free to spend them in dancing attendance on the Court: nay, were not free to do otherwise. The century began with the French monarchy triumphant over all its great vassals; it finished by reducing all its vassals, great and small, to the condition of courtiers, with little influence in the country-side, and diminished rents—mere absentee landlords of the worst type, endowed with privileges which could only be exercised at the cost of the starvation of the people and the exasperation of the Bourgeoisie, who furnished the funds for the Court glory. Everything in France, therefore, foreshadowed political revolution. What the advancing constitutionalism of England foreshadowed we shall have to speak of in our next chapter.

Chapter V

PREPARING FOR REVOLUTION— ENGLAND

The English seventeenth century revolution was from the first purely middle-class, and as we hinted in our last it cast off most of its elements of enthusiasm and ideality in Cromwell's latter days; the burden of the more exalted Puritanism was felt heavily by the nation and no doubt played its part in the restoration of Monarchy; nor on the other hand was England at all ripe for Republicanism; and so between these two disgusts it allowed itself to be led back again into the arms of Monarchy by the military adventurers who had seized on the power which Cromwell once wielded. But this restoration of the Stuart monarchy was after all but a makeshift put up with because the defection from the high-strung principle of the earlier period of the revolution left nothing to take the place of Cromwell's absolutism. The nation was quite out of sympathy with the Court, which was un-national and Catholic in tendency and quite openly debauched. The nation itself though it had got rid of the severity of Puritanism was still Puritan, and welcomed the Sunday Act of Charles II. which gave the due legal stamp to Puritanism of the duller and more respectable kind. And though enthusiastic Puritanism was no longer dominant, it was not extinct. John Bunyan's "Pilgrim's Progress" shines out, though a religious romance, amidst the dulness of the literature of the time. The Quakers who represented in their beginning the peaceable and religious side of the Levellers, arose and grew and flourished in spite of persecution; the Cameronians in Scotland, as we mentioned in our last chapter, made an ineffectual armed resistance to the dying out of enthusiasm; while across the Atlantic the descendants of the earlier Puritans carried on an almost theocratic government, which, by the way be it said, persecuted the Quakers most cruelly. Little by little, however, all that was not quite commonplace and perfunctory, died out in English Protestantism, and respectable indifferentism had carried all before it by the end of the century. Politics and religion had no longer any real bond of union, and the religious side of Protestantism, Evangelicalism, disappears here, to come to light again in the next century under the leadership of Whitfield.

Yet, such as English Puritanism had become, its respectable, habitual, and formal residuum was strong enough to resent James the Second's Papistry, and to make its resentment felt; while at the same time the constitutionalism which began the anti-absolutist opposition in Charles the First's time, and which had been interrupted by Cromwell's iron and Charles the Second's mud absolutism, gathered head again and began to take definite form. The Stuart monarchy, with its "divine right" of absolute sovereignty, was driven from England in the person of James the Second, and a constitutional king was found in William of Orange, and constitutional party government began.

Thus, in spite of interruption, was carried out the middle-class revolution in England; like all other revolutions, it arrived at the point which it really set out to gain; but not until it had shaken off much which did at one time help forward its progress, and which was and still is mistaken for an essential part of it. Religious and Republican enthusiasm, although they (and especially the first) played their part in abolishing the reactionary clogs on the progress of the middle-classes, had to disappear as elements which would have marred the end proposed by that revolution; to wit, the creation of an all-powerful middle-class freed from all restrictions that would interfere with it in its pursuit of individual profit derived from the exploitation of industry.

Thenceforth, till our own times, respectable political life in England is wrapped up in Whiggery; tinged, indeed, on one side with the last faint remains of feudalism in the form of a quite unreal sentiment, involving no practical consequences but the acceptance of the name of Tory; and on the other by as faint a sentiment towards democracy, which was probably rather a traditional survival of the feeling of the old days of the struggle between King and Parliament, than any holding out of the hand towards the real democracy which was silently forming underneath the government of the respectables.

The first part of the eighteenth century, therefore, finds England solid and settled; all the old elements of disturbance and aspiration hardened into constitutional bureaucracy; religion recognised as a State formality, but having no influence whatever on the corporate life of the country, its sole reality a mere personal sentiment, not at all burdensome to the practical business of life. The embers of the absolutist re-action on the point of extinction, and swept off easily and even lazily when they make a show of being dangerous; the nobility a mere titled upper order of the bourgeoisie; the country prosperous, gaining on French and on Dutch in America and India, and beginning to found its colonial and foreign markets, and its navy beginning to be paramount on all seas; the working-classes better off than at any time since the fifteenth century. Art if not actually dead represented by a Court painter or so of ugly ladies and stupid gentlemen, and literature by a few word-spinning essayists and prosaic versifiers, priding themselves on a well-bred contempt for whatever was manly, passionate, or elevating in the wealth of the past of their own language.

Here then in England we may begin to see what the extinction of feudality was to end in. Mediæval England is gone, the manners and ways of thought of the people are utterly changed; they are called English, by they are another people from that which dwelt in England when "forestalling and regratting" were misdemeanours; when the gild ruled over the production of goods and division of labour was not yet; when both in art and literature the people had their share,—nay, when what of both there was, was produced by the people themselves. Gone also is militant Puritanism, buried deep under mountains of cool formality. England is bourgeois and successful throughout its whole life; without aspirations, for its self-satisfaction is too complete for any, yet gathering force for development of a new kind,—as it were a nation taking breath for a new spring; for under its prosperous self-satisfaction lies the birth of a great change—a revolution in industry—and England is at the time we are writing of simply preparing herself for that change. Her prosperity and solid bureaucratic constitutional government—nay, even the commonplace conditions of life in the country, are enabling her to turn all her attention towards this change, and the development of the natural resources in which she is so rich. The fall of the feudal system, the invasion of the individualist method of producing goods, and of simple exchange of commodities, were bound to lead to the final development of the epoch—the rise of the great machine industries—and now the time for that development is at hand. The growing world-market is demanding more than the transitional methods of production can supply. In matters political prejudice is giving way to necessity, and all obstacles are being rapidly cleared away before the advent of a new epoch for labour; of which, indeed, we may say that if no great change were at hand for it in its turn, it would have been the greatest disaster which has ever happened to the race of man....

Chapter IX

THE INDUSTRIAL REVOLUTION
IN ENGLAND

... In the last chapter wherein the condition of England was dealt with, we left it a prosperous country, in the ordinary sense of the world, under the rule of an orderly constitutionalism. There was no need here for the violent destruction of aristocratic privilege; it was of itself melting into money-privilege, and all was getting ready for the completest and securest system of the plunder of labour which the world had yet seen.

England was free in the bourgeois sense; that is, there were but a few checks, the survivals of earlier periods, to interfere with the exaction of the tribute which labour has to pay to property to be allowed to live. In a word, on the one hand exploitation was veiled; and on the other, the owners of property had no longer any duties to perform in return for the above-said tribute. Nevertheless, all this had to go on on a small scale for a while. Population had not increased largely since the beginning of the seventeenth century; agriculture was flourishing; one-thirtieth of the grain raised was exported from England; the working-classes were not hard pressed, and could not yet be bought and sold in masses. There were no large manufacturing towns, and no need for them; the presence of the material to be worked up, rather than the means for working it mechanically—fuel, to wit—gave a manufacturing character to this or that country-side. It was, for example, the sheep-pastures of the Yorkshire hill-sides, and not the existence of coal beneath them, which made the neighbourhood of the (*sic*) northern Bradford a weaving country. Its namesake on the Wiltshire Avon was in those days at least as important a centre of the clothing industry. The broadcloth of the Gloucestershire valleys, Devonshire and Hampshire kersies, Whitney blankets and Chipping Norton tweeds, meant sweet grass and long wool, with a little water-power to turn the fulling-mills, and not coal, to which material to be worked up was to be brought from the four quarters of the globe. The apparent condition of labour in those days seems almost idyllic, compared with what it now is: but it must be remembered that then as now the worker was in the hands of the monopolist of land and raw material; nor was it likely that the latter should have held his special privilege for two hundred years without applying some system by which it could be made the most of. Between the period of the decay of the craft-gilds and this latter half of the eighteenth century there had grown up a system of labour which could not have been applied to the mediæval workmen; for they worked for themselves and not for a master or exploiter, and thus were masters of their material and their tools and their time. This system is that of the Division of Labour; under it the unit of labour is not an individual man, but a group, every member of which is helpless by himself, but trained by constant practice to the repetition of a small part of the work, acquires great precision and speed in its performance. In short, each man is not so much a machine as a part of a machine. As, for example, it takes five men to make a glass-bottle: it is the group of these five men that makes the bottle, not any one of them. It is clear that under this system the individual workman is entirely at the mercy of his master the capitalist in his capacity of superintender of labour: in order not to be crushed by him, he must combine to oppose his own interests to those of his employer. It was by this system, then, that the demands of the growing world-market were supplied down to the end of the eighteenth century. The great political economist, Adam Smith, whose book was first published in 1771, marks the beginning of the transition between this system and that of the great machine industries; but his work implies throughout the Division of Labour system.

But that system was now to melt into the new one: the workman, from being a machine, was to become the auxiliary of a machine. The invention of the spinning-jenny by Hargreaves in 1760 is the first symptom of the beginning of this Industrial Revolution. From thence to the invention of steam as a motive-force, and thence again to our own days, the stream of invention has been continuous. The discovery that iron could be made with pit-coal removed the seat of the iron manufacture from the wooded countries of the south and west, where the old iron-works, called "bloomeries," used to be carried on, to the northern and midland coal districts, and all manufacturer of any importance flowed to the seat of fuel; so that South Lancashire, for instance, was changed from a country of moorland and pasture, with a few market towns and the ancient manufacturing city of Manchester, into a district where the "villages," still so called, but with populations of fifteen or twenty thousand souls, are pretty much contiguous, and the country has all but disappeared. Of course a great part of this is the work of the years that have followed on the invention of railways; but even in the earlier period of this industrial revolution the change was tremendous and sudden and the sufferings of the working classes very great, as no attempt was made to alleviate the distress that was sure to be caused by the change from the use of human hands to machinery. Nor indeed could it have been made in a country governed by bourgeois constitutionalism until measures were actually forced on the government. In 1811 the prevailing distress was betokened by the first outbreak of the Luddites. These were organised bands of men who went about breaking up the machinery which was the immediate cause of their want of employment and consequent starvation. The locality where these riots were most frequent was the northern midland counties, where the newly-invented stocking-frames were specially obnoxious to them. The Luddites became the type of bodies of rioters who by a half-blind instinct throughout this period threw themselves against the advancing battalions of industrial revolution. In 1816, the year which followed the peace with France, the cessation of all the war industries threw more people still out of employment, and in addition the harvest was a specially bad one. As a consequence, this hunger insurrection was especially violent in that year. The riots were put down with corresponding violence, and the rioters punished with the utmost harshness. But as times mended somewhat this insurrection, which was, as we have said, a mere matter of hunger, and was founded on no principle, died out, although for a time riots having for their object destruction of property, especially of the plant and stock of manufacturers, went on through the whole of the first half of the century. The "Plug Riots,"[1] in the middle of the Chartist agitation, may be taken for an example of these.

It was a necessary consequence of the introduction of elaborate machinery that women and children should be largely employed in factories to diminish the number of adult males. This resource for the development of the profits of the new system was used by the manufacturers with the utmost recklessness, till at last it became clear to the bourgeois government that the scandal created by its abuse would put an end to its use altogether, unless something were done to palliate its immediate evils; and accordingly a series of Factory Acts were passed, in the teeth of the most strenuous and unscrupulous resistance on the part of the capitalists, who grudged the immediate loss which resulted in the hampering of the "roaring trade" they were driving, even though it were for the ultimate benefit of their class. The first of these Acts which was really intended to work was passed in 1830, and they were consolidated finally in 1867. It should be understood that these Acts were not intended to benefit the great mass of adult workers, but were rather concessions to the outcry of the philanthropists at the condition of the women and especially the children so employed. Meanwhile, in spite of all the suffering caused by the Industrial Revolution, it was impossible for the capitalists to engross the whole of the profits gained by it, or at least to go on piling them up in an ever-increasing ratio. The class struggle took another form, besides that of mere hunger riots and forcible repression, that of the Trade Unions. Although the primary intention of these was the foundation of benefit societies, as with the first guilds of the early Middle Ages, like them also they had soon to take in hand matters dealing with the regulation of labour. The first struggles of the trades' unions with capital took place while they were still illegal; but the repeal of the law against the combination of workmen in 1824 set them free in that respect, and they soon began to be a power in the country. Aided by the rising tide of commercial prosperity, which made the capitalists more willing to yield up some part of their enormous profits rather than carry on the struggle *à l'outrance*, they prevailed in many trade contests, and succeeding (*sic*) in raising the standard of livelihood for skilled workmen, though of course by no means in proportion to the huge increase in the sum of the national income. Further than this it was and is impossible for them to go on so long as they recognise the capitalists as a necessary part of the organisation of labour. It was not at first understood by the capitalist class that they did so recognise them, and consequently in the period of their early successes the trades' unions were considered mere revolutionists, and were treated to that kind of virulent and cowardly abuse and insult, which the shopkeeper in terror for his shop always has at his tongue['']s end.

The abolition of the corn-laws in 1847 and the consequent cheapening of necessary food for the workers, the discovery of

gold in California and Australia, the prodigious increase in the
luxury and expenditure of the upper and middle classes, all the
action and reaction of the commercial impulse created by the
great machine industries, gave an appearance of general prosperity to the country, in which, as we have said, the skilled workmen
did partake to a certain extent; and the views of middle-class
optimists as to the continuance of bourgeois progress, and the
gradual absorption of all the worthy part of the working-classes
into its ranks seemed confirmed till within the last few years; all
the more as the practical triumph of the Liberal party had ceased
to make "politics" a burning question. Nevertheless, as a sign that
the underground lava had not ceased flowing, it was noticed that
ever since the ripening of the great industries, in periods of about
ten years came recurring depressions of trade; these were
accounted for in various ingenious ways, but otherwise did not
trouble the capitalist mind, which got to consider this also,
because of its regular recurrence, as a sign of the stability of the
present system, and merely looked upon it as a thing to be taken
into the general average and insured against in the usual manner.
But within the last few years this latest eternal bourgeois provi-
dence has failed us. The nations whom we assumed would never
do anything but provide us with raw materials, have become our
rivals in manufacture and our competitors in the world-market,
while owing to the fact that America has enormous stretches of
easily tilled virgin soil, which does not need manure, and that the
climate of India makes it easy to support life there, those two
countries supply us with such large amounts of grain, and at so
cheap a rate, that raising it in England has become unprofitable;
so that the farmers are poor, and the landlords cannot get the
same rents for agricultural land as formerly. The exports have
fallen off; towns where six years ago trade was flourishing and
wages high, are now encumbered with a population which they
cannot find employment for; and though from time to time there
are rumours of improvement in trade, nothing comes of them,

and people are obliged to wait some stroke of magic which shall bring us back our old prosperity "of leaps and bounds."

The fact is that the commerce of the great industries has entered insensibly into its second stage, and mere cut-throat competition between the different nations has taken the place of the benevolent commercial despotism of the only nation which was thoroughly prepared to take advantage of the Industrial Revolution—Great Britain, to wit.

The second stage is doubtless preparing the final one which will end with the death of the whole bourgeois commercial system. Meanwhile, what is the real social product of the Industrial Revolution? We answer the final triumph of the middle-classes, materially, intellectually, and morally. As the result of the great political revolution in France was the abolition of aristocratic privilege, and the domination in the world of politics of the bourgeoisie, which hitherto had had little to do with it, so the English Industrial Revolution may be said to have created a new commercial middle-class hitherto unknown to the world. This class on the one hand consolidated all the groups of the middle class of the preceding epoch, such as country squires large and small, big farmers, merchants, manufacturers, shopkeepers, and professional men; and made them so conscious of their solidarity, that the ordinary refined and thinking man of to-day cannot really see any other class at all, but only outside his own class certain heterogeneous groups to be used as instruments for the further advancement of that class. On the other hand, it has attained such complete domination that the upper classes are merely adjuncts to it and servants of it. In fact, these also are now of the bourgeois class as they are all engaged in commerce in one way or other: *e.g.*, the higher nobility are all either house-agents or coal-factors, and would be of no importance without their "businesses." Moreover, striving ever to extend itself downwards as well as upwards, the middle-class has absorbed so much in that direction, especially within the last thirty years, that it has

now nothing left below it except the mere propertyless proletariat. These last are wholly dependent upon it, utterly powerless
before it until the break up of the system which has created it,
the signs of whose beginning we have just noted, shall *force* them
into a revolt against it. In the course of that revolt this great
middle-class will in its turn be absorbed into the proletariat,
which will form a new Society in which classes will have ceased
to exist. This is the next Revolution, as inevitable, as inexorable,
as the rising of to-morrow's sun.

1   This meant destruction of boilers in factories, the rioters pulling out the
    plugs to ensure their bursting.

SELECT BIBLIOGRAPHY AND FURTHER READING

i) Editions of Morris's own works

Boos, F. (ed.), *William Morris's Socialist Diary* (London: The Journeyman Press, 1985).

Henderson, P. (ed.), *The Letters of William Morris to his Family and Friends* (London: Longmans, 1950).

Kelvin, N. (ed.), *The Collected Letters of William Morris* (4 vols, Princeton, NJ: Princeton University Press, 1984-96).

LeMire, E. (ed.), *The Unpublished Lectures of William Morris* (Detroit: Wayne State University Press, 1969).

Morris, M. (ed.), *The Collected Works of William Morris* (24 vols, London: Longman, Green & Co., 1910-15).

—(ed.), *William Morris: Artist, Writer, Socialist* (2 vols, Oxford: Basil Blackwell, 1936).

Peterson, W.S. (ed.), *The Ideal Book: Essays and Lectures on the Arts of the Book by William Morris* (Berkeley: University of California Press, 1982).

Salmon, N. (ed.), *Political Writings* (Bristol: Thoemmes Press, 1994).

—(ed.), *Journalism* (Bristol: Thoemmes Press, 1996).

ii) Biographies and surveys

Bradley, I., *William Morris and his World* (London: Thames & Hudson, 1978).

Dore, H., *William Morris* (London: Pyramid, 1990).

Faulkner, P. (ed.), *William Morris: The Critical Heritage* (London: Routledge & Kegan Paul, 1973).

—*Against the Age: An Introduction to William Morris* (London: Allen & Unwin, 1980).

Glasier, J.B., *William Morris and the Early Days of the Socialist Movement* (London: Longmans, Green & Co., 1921).

Henderson, P., *William Morris: His Life, Work and Friends* (London, Thames & Hudson, 1967).

Lindsay, J., *William Morris: His Life & Works* (London: Constable, 1975).

MacCarthy, F., *William Morris: A Life for Our Time* (London: Faber & Faber, 1994).

Mackail, J.W., *The Life and Work of William Morris* (2 vols, London: Longmans, 1899).

Poulson, C., *William Morris* (London: The Apple Press, 1989).

Thompson, E.P., *William Morris: Romantic to Revolutionary* (London: Lawrence & Wishart, 1955).

Thompson, P., *The Work of William Morris* (London: Heinemann, 1967).

Vallance, A., *William Morris: His Art, his Writings and his Public Life* (London: George Bell & Sons, 1897).

iii) Works on Morris's family and friends

Burne-Jones, G., *Memorials of Edward Burne-Jones* (2 vols, London: Macmillan, 1904).

Cowley, J., *The Victorian Encounter with Marx: A Study of Ernest Belfort Bax* (London: British Academic Press, 1992).

Faulkner, P. (ed.), *Jane Morris to Wilfrid Scawen Blunt* (Exeter: University of Exeter, 1986).

Fitzgerald, P., *Edward Burne-Jones: A Biography* (London: Michael Joseph, 1975).

Lethaby, W.R., *Philip Webb and his Work* (London: Oxford University Press, 1935).

Marsh, J., *Jane and May Morris: A Biographical Story 1839–1938* (London: Pandora, 1986).

iv) Other important works

Arnot, R.P., *William Morris: A Vindication* (London: Martin Lawrence, 1934).

—*William Morris: The Man and the Myth* (London: Lawrence & Wishart, 1964).

Banham, J. & Harris, J. (eds.), *William Morris and the Middle Ages* (Manchester: Manchester University Press, 1984).

Clark, F., *William Morris: Wallpapers and Chintzes* (London: Academy Editions, 1974).

Cockerell, S. (ed.), *A Note by William Morris on his aims in founding the Kelmscott Press, together with a short history of the press* (London: Kelmscott Press, 1898).

Fairclough, O. & Leary, E., *Textiles by William Morris and Co. 1861–1940* (London: Thames & Hudson, 1981).

Harvey, C. & Press, J., *William Morris, Design and Enterprise in Victorian Britain* (Manchester: Manchester University Press, 1991).

Hodgson, A., *The Romances of William Morris* (London: Cambridge University Press, 1987).

Meier, P., *William Morris: The Marxist Dreamer* (Sussex: Harvester Press, 1978).

Needham, P., *William Morris and the Art of the Book* (London: Oxford University Press, 1976).

Oberg, C., *A Pagan Prophet: William Morris* (Charlottesville: University Press of Virginia, 1978).

Parry, L., *William Morris Textiles* (London: Weidenfeld & Nicolson, 1983).

Peterson, W.S., *The Kelmscott Press: A History of William Morris's Typographical Adventure* (Oxford: Clarendon Press, 1989).

Pevsner, N., *Pioneers of the Modern Movement* (London: Faber & Faber, 1936).

Robinson, D., *William Morris, Burne-Jones and the Kelmscott Chaucer* (London: Fraser, 1982).

Robinson, R., & Wildman, S., *Morris and Company in Cambridge* (Cambridge: Cambridge University Press, 1980).

Sewter, A.C., *The Stained Glass of William Morris and his Circle* (2 vols, New Haven: Yale University Press, 1974–75).

Sparling, H.H., *The Kelmscott Press and William Morris Master-Craftsman* (London: Macmillan, 1924).

Stansky, P., *Redesigning the World: William Morris, the 1880s and the Arts and Crafts Movement* (Princeton NJ: Princeton University Press, 1985).

Watkinson, R., *William Morris as Designer* (London: Studio Vista, 1967).

THE WILLIAM MORRIS SOCIETY

The life, work and ideas of William Morris are as important today as they were in his lifetime. *The William Morris Society* exists to make them as widely known as possible.

The many-sidedness of Morris and the variety of his activities bring together in the *Society* those who are interested in him as designer, craftsman, businessman, poet, socialist, or who admire his robust and generous personality, his creative energy and courage. Morris aimed for a state of affairs in which all might enjoy the potential richness of human life. His thought on how we might live, on creative work, leisure and machinery, on ecology and conservation, on the place of the arts in our lives and their relation to politics, as on much else, remains as challenging now as it was a century ago. He provides a focus for those who deplore the progressive dehumanization of the world in the twentieth-century and who believe, with him, that the trend is not inevitable.

The *Society* provides information on topics of interest to its members and arranges lectures, visits, exhibitions and other events. It encourages the reprinting of his works and the continued manufacture of his textile and wallpaper designs. It publishes a journal twice a year, free to members, which carries articles across the field of Morris scholarship. It also publishes a quarterly newsletter giving details of its programme, new publications and other matters of interest concerning Morris and his circle. Members are invited to contribute items both to the journal and to the newsletter. *The William Morris Society* has a world-wide membership and offers the chance to make contact with fellow Morrisians both in Britain and abroad.

Regular events include a Kelmscott Lecture, a birthday party held in March, and visits to exhibitions and such places as the William Morris Gallery, Red House, Kelmscott Manor and Standen. These visits, our tours and our short residential study courses, enable members living abroad or outside London to participate in the *Society's* activities. The *Society* also has local groups in various parts of Britain and affiliated Societies in the USA and Canada.

For further details, write to:

The Hon. Membership Secretary, Kelmscott House, 26 Upper Mall, Hammersmith, London W6 9TA.